CW00971885

YOU CAN GET THERE

R PRESTON TODD

BALBOA
PRESS

A DIVISION OF HAY HOUSE

Balboa Press books may be ordered through booksellers or by contacting:

Balboa Press
A Division of Hay House
1663 Liberty Drive
Bloomington, IN 47403
www.balboapress.com
1 (877) 407-4847

Because of the dynamic nature of the Internet, any web addresses or
links contained in this book may have changed since publication and
may no longer be valid. The views expressed in this work are solely those
of the author and do not necessarily reflect the views of the publisher,
and the publisher hereby disclaims any responsibility for them.

The author of this book does not dispense medical advice or prescribe the use
of any technique as a form of treatment for physical, emotional, or medical
problems without the advice of a physician, either directly or indirectly. The
intent of the author is only to offer information of a general nature to help
you in your quest for emotional and spiritual well-being. In the event you use
any of the information in this book for yourself, which is your constitutional
right, the author and the publisher assume no responsibility for your actions.

Any people depicted in stock imagery provided by Thinkstock are models,
and such images are being used for illustrative purposes only.
Certain stock imagery © Thinkstock.

Print information available on the last page.

ISBN: 978-1-5043-9237-2 (sc)
ISBN: 978-1-5043-9238-9 (hc)
ISBN: 978-1-5043-9239-6 (e)

Library of Congress Control Number: 2017918154

Balboa Press rev. date: 11/30/2017

PROLOGUE

The Universe has been around for a long, long time.

- The Universe has been around longer than Rs / Ds (or any kind of political party)
- The Universe has been around longer than Capitalism (or any other kind of Economics)
- The Universe has been around longer than America (or Europe)
- The Universe has been around longer than Monarchies (or any other kind of ruling body)
- The Universe has been around longer than religion (or any other kind of philosophy)
- The Universe has been around longer than Plato (or any kind of Utopia)
- The Universe has been around longer than Earth itself (billions and billions of years)

So let's just say ... the Universe has been around for a long, long time. Once you include the concept of time, further discussion becomes logical, rational, or left-brained (for right-handed people, or those whose "dominant" side is their right).

Universe does more than simply stand for singular, it has the "Uni" part right in it! "Multiverse" does more than just imply greater than one in the same manner. Assuming we have multiple *Realities*, maybe each one gets its own Universe. Who knows? Who cares? *Raise your hand! You have been promoted to an honorary Trekkie, if you are not a Trekkie already!*

We'll forget the person going to their therapist saying "I have this friend who …" Whether or not that person really *is* the friend is irrelevant. Some people are their own best friend, because they have yet to get a doG. *I usually capitalize the "G" in doG not just to confuse my smell checker, but because doG is God spelled backwards (uppercase "G" with unconditional love added. "Smell checker" makes it completely like a doG).*

All the different words used for God refer to the same thing in someone's mental dictionary, but here we'll try to use the "G" word as infrequently as possible. Some have no problem with the "G" word, but elsewhere it's used inconsistently, so *"Infinity"* is often used instead; there is no place it is not. If you note a similarity to how some define the "G" word, so be it.

In a dialog with a childhood friend, I noted she was lucky to have never been dragged to "church" by her parents. She said she did not have religion nor spirituality, and would not know what spirituality would look like regardless. It seemed clear she equated them.

I do NOT have religion, but I definitely have spirituality, and this dialog caused me to think: what *IS* spirituality, and what does it look like? Certainly "spirituality" is not the type triggered and later monopolized by religion. Read on for the simple definition of spirituality.

"In the Beginning … God." (Whoever wrote this in **The Bible** used the "G" word.) So starts the most famous writing in Judea-Christian history, which is also the best-selling book by far, even though most do not understand it, or read beyond the first few pages. Presently, it is still cool to have on your bookshelf.

Religion, coming from *Infinity*, would normally require no words nor explanations; but **The Bible** (and western religion) is followed by hundreds, if not thousands, of pages of words and explanations for everything from light, to the number 12, to the seven days in the week. **The Bible** itself is printed on extra thin paper, while some explanations are divinely sublime (*check out the rhyme*).

These words and explanations have caused many people, some believe, to live a more moral life. There are even rules-to-live-by, called commandments (carved in stone) because if there weren't, people would go around murdering *and coveting* at will. Now lawyer-politicians have taken over laws / commandments from religion. There used to be only one commandment about murder ("Thy shalt not murder" [you know it is religious because of the "thy" and "shalt" parts]). The commandment has now become multiple laws when lawyers take over: 1st degree, 2nd degree, 3rd degree murder, PLUS manslaughter. Neither the commandment, nor subsequent laws, say anything about "kill," *so I guess killing is OK.*

There are Ten Commandments, making them easy-to-remember ... well, at least the number ten is easy to remember. If you are a student of American history, you will note ten is the same number as the original Constitution's "Bill of Rights" which was promised by politicians to get states to ratify it. Whether the number ten is a coincidence, you be the judge. *Politicians are, to a large degree, lawyers, so they are well paid, vote themselves a raise when they think no one is looking, then go on vacation, and no longer actually do anything they promise.*

When I first realized one of my quests was to find an explanation of how things get here, I also realized instructions would be without words and simply work. My reasoning went: who would have been around to teach anyone how to write down and follow any instructions? *Men in black robes – be they priests, lawyers, or judges – have always been around. So has hell and the devil (and lawyers-from-hell).*

Religions evolve, and so did I, going from Christianity into New Thought, and on from there. In the interim, landing in a New Thought Religion "church" (Religious Science / Science of Mind [SOM]), there I found other people of like mind, and did a lot of reading, learning, and classes were attended.

The textbook definition of New Thought merges religion and science together, and it says things that *appear* are going on *in your mind first.* You are probably familiar with some New Thought Religions such as Christian Science (thanks to their NEWSpaper – ***The Christian Science Monitor***. They even have "reading rooms" where you can go to read their NEWSpaper!) Unity and Religious Science are some other New Thought Religions.

Religious Science, too, contains buzz-words that need explanation, but there are less of them, and at least it didn't take thin paper to explain **subjective** and **objective**, although the explanations were dated and contained writing consistent with the 1800s. Somewhat satisfied, I kept an open mind toward the goal in which **NO WORDS** are required to make the divine creative force work, which encompasses most religions.

As the pendulum swings, predictions have it the pendulum will now swing back in the direction of religion, because it has now swung too far in the direction of science. We now have formulas and predictions for everything; if we don't already have them, we will soon!

Where did I go? Going from Carlos Castaneda's Yaqui Indians "A Way of Knowledge" into Zen Buddhism and other Far East "Religions," and ho'oponopono which migrated to Hawaii in advance of any "western" anything, eventually I arrived back at Hebrew and Christian philosophy; although speaking of western, there is an almost complete ignorance of Muslim tradition, which is supposed to be western. Daniel Lapin (a Rabbi and speaker) writing ***Business Secrets from the Bible*** finished my learning.

Probing deeper, the Law of Attraction and Quantum Physics were moved through, all of which lead to the following explanations given here, and eventually I included "free thinking." A lot of channeled wisdom is involved, including Pathwork (emotional maturity), Seth, and what is currently known as the Law of Attraction (Abraham). The resultant explanation requires **NO WORDS** for the Universe to work (right-brain), but **WORDS** are used to communicate and somewhat understand it (left-brain).

PREFACE

On *Hawaii 5-0*, they were replaying an episode in which the name on the stern of a boat was "ho'oponopono." Since there are no coincidences, I immediately re-read the book *Zero Limits* [1] which detailed the ho'oponopono philosophy; it migrated to Hawaii from islands in the South Pacific along with the move to Hawaii, and was later modernized. **Michener** and *Hawaii* [2] have more about the discovery and settlement of the islands, so you can read more about Hawaii from the very beginning of the earth if you care to. *Anyone that has read some of Michener's works knows about "from the very beginning."*

After Dr. Wayne Dyer passed, I repetitively re-watched the part in *Wisdom of the Ages* (a PBS TV fundraiser) which detailed Wayne's experience with a Monarch Butterfly. That part was soo funny, but I knew there was more. I found Dr. Dyer's book (it has the picture of him on the front with the butterfly), and it explored synchronicity. Such is synchronicity in *Life*, as well as living an inspired ("in spirit") life.

---

[1] Vitale, Joe; Len, Ihaleakala Hew. Zero Limits: The Secret Hawaiian System for Wealth, Health, Peace, and More (all pages). Wiley. Kindle Edition.
[2] Michener, James. Hawaii: A Novel (all pages). Random House Publishing Group. Kindle Edition.

You would be well advised to "Live in spirit" by embracing *Reality*. Therefore the saying is: "You are a spiritual being having a human experience" and NOT "You are a human having a spiritual experience." Live in spirit. Live an inspired *Life*. [3]

CAN is often capitalized (among some other words in this book) as if shouting them, like in eMail. The AM part of "I AM" is accordingly capitalized – you can read more about it in other writings [4]. I AM extremely careful about what I follow AM with, since it expresses your link to *Infinity*. In some languages like ancient Hebrew, it is illegal to use this term, maybe for this reason. *In the ancient Hebrew language, the phrase translates to something like "I AM what I AM."*

You might consider what is detailed within a mental discipline. You will also find out more about it in **The Way It Is** which claimed NOT to have any specific instructions. But you need only follow the instructions given carefully here; such is the only necessary discipline.

You can take generic directions, and make them specific, but that was not the intention of that book. But it IS the intention here to give specific instructions, like a cookbook or diet. If you don't lose weight, that's not the fault of the cookbook or the diet. You just haven't had the discipline to FOLLOW THE INSTRUCTIONS! *Maybe you substituted chocolate when the recipe does not call for it!*

Of course, many will follow the instructions for a while, then give up … you just haven't followed the instructions LONG ENOUGH, or CAREFULLY ENOUGH! What, do you think you are going to lose those extra pounds by following the instructions for a week? How

---

[3] Dyer, Wayne W. Inspiration: Your Ultimate Calling (p. 175). Hay House. Kindle Edition.

[4] Dyer, Wayne W.; Tracy, Kristina. I Am: Why Two Little Words Mean So Much (Kindle Locations: all). Hay House. Kindle Edition.

long did it take the extra pounds to get there? I am *not* suggesting it would take as long to shed the extra pounds as it took them to get there, but it will probably take longer than a week to get rid of them. The same goes for giving up smoking, drinking, *et al. It's your parent's fault anyway!*

> *What about Love?*
> *Don't let it slip away*
> **Heart; *What about Love***

But ***Don't Worry Baby***, you can't let *Love* slip away! Going back in time even further was the song ***Don't Worry Baby*** by the **Beach Boys**. We'll make some very minor changes to the first lines in the quote – actually a minor change is made only to the first line – and make the two lines apply to *Infinite Love* as well as "puppy love" (my term for the usual usage of "Love.") *Of course, he usually whispers in her ear "I Love You"* and NOT *"I puppy love you."*

The line in the song we're going to change starts with "She." You can make that "He" if you want it to be the unisex version (because God is usually male), just remember to capitalize the first letter, especially in the unisex version. It goes:

> *She told me "Baby when you're racin' then just take along my love with you*
> *"And if you knew how much I love you baby nothin' could go wrong with you"*
> **The Beach Boys; *Don't Worry Baby***

Then change "She" to the "G" word (if you want) and replace "racing" with whatever you want. Now the two lines read:

> *God told me "Baby when you're <doing whatever> then just take along my **Love** with you*

> *"And if you knew how much I **Love** you baby nothin' could go wrong with you"*

There, it's done! Nothing can go wrong, and you can't get away from taking **Love** (aka *Life* or *The Power of Creation*) along anyway, nor can you get away without taking spirituality along. So it would seem you can't get away from taking *Love, Infinity, Reality* along too. The Power of Creation, *Life*, and Spirituality as well as many other synonyms, are taken along also, but let's not get too complicated. *Leave the thousands of explanations for someone else.*

Speaking of something where there is nowhere it isn't (like the "G" word) try "Love" on for size. The ***Course in Miracles*** tells us:

> *You have but two emotions, and one you made and one was given you* [5]

Love is one of those two-sided words. It both represents: the nearest word one can use to express the creative process used by *Infinity*, along with "puppy love" (being in love with someone *whereby you can listen non-stop to the love song channel on AM radio – but who could explain* that *anyway*).

Because it's the most common, puppy love is the one most refer to, and yields such ridiculous euphemisms as "making love" with someone you could care less about – it's really just sex. A non-euphemistic usage of the term "making love" unites the two meanings, even though "practitioners" are probably unaware of both parts! Sometimes people who are really "in love" just have sex. Everything will not only turn out alright, but it already *IS*.

---

[5] Schucman, Helen (2011-05-06). A Course in Miracles: Original Edition (Kindle Locations 6485-6486). White Crow Books. Kindle Edition.

You brought only one emotion here with you, and that is "Love" – the creative kind. If you made any emotion, you made "fear," then all kinds of other emotions out of them. "You can't take it with you" is almost true, but you do take the same creative love with which you came.

In case you're in-the-mood for something more current than the Beach Boys or Heart:

> *I wanna know what love is; I want you to show me*
> *I wanna feel what love is; I know you can show me*
> **Foreigner; *I Wanna Know what Love Is***

Which type Love do you think *that* is (*Infinite*, Puppy, or both)?

> *I can't complain but sometimes I still do*
> *Life's been good to me so far*
> **Joe Walsh; *Life's Been Good to Me***

You can get the complete version of these songs through Google or YouTube! By-the-Way (*or BTW for young-uns*) you might want to check out the video on YouTube! regarding the **Bee Gees** and *Stayin Alive* – especially the dude singing falsetto – because he is *Stayin Alive* no longer.

We're only here for a relatively short time (*regardless of however long* **John Travolta** *aka Vinnie Barbarino seems to be around*), especially when you consider how long eternity is. They say "You can't take it with you," but you *do* return with the only thing you brought along: *Love* – the creative kind. There is no further need for any definition of spirituality when in *Reality* you're alive no longer and have returned to *Infinity*, but you'll always have *Love*.

We will start by tuning up on *Infinity*, *Reality*, and *Life*. You can research *Infinity*, and read about *Realities*, but you need go no farther than here. Words can only allude to *Infinity*, and you are already in a *Reality* of your own making, so you really need go no farther. *Life* comes along as a referee, who dictates the rules regarding what is physical or not.

If you normally can't follow instructions, then these instructions are designed to be easy to follow for more than a week. JUST FOLLOW THEM! Capitalizing something IS shouting it.

You CAN Get There from here!

WHAT'S NEW?

In **You CAN Get There**, items looked at differently than usual, or are brand-new include:

- The three "pieces of existence" are given the labels: *Infinity, Reality,* and *Life*
- *Life* acts as a referee between *Infinity* and *Reality*
- Your *Reality* is determined by *Life*, before you return to *Infinity*
- Spirituality is NOT GIVEN by religion. Here we have a simple explanation
- Many coined terms ("Free thinking") are used and enclosed in quotes when first used
- Some "consciousness entities" provide help while NOT "in body"
- Other consciousness entities take on form to potentially learn lessons
- "Inside" vs. "Outside" (the factors in the formation of beliefs)
- "Creationism" is the word we assign to this philosophy
- The *Multi-dimensional Roadmap-of-Life* (introduced in *The Way It Is*) is used to select and migrate to a new position, from a presumably unsatisfactory one
  - o Easy to follow
  - o Using personal examples from the author

Song entries, mostly "old" and unknown for youngsters, many even "old" to old-timers, are continued to be used to illustrate points, but there are no "classics" from Frank Sinatra. *Maybe I should have included "New York, New York!"*

> *Song Verse #1 is formatted accordingly*
> *Song Verse #2*
> **Popular Song author; *Song***

Explanations using words and apropos definitions are added to a Glossary at the end for those not familiar with a word, or how it is used here. The Glossary is there to assist anyone new to the subject, as well as certain terms with which you might not be familiar, especially in the context used. It is extensive, so you may want to start by reviewing it to see what concepts might be new (and coined terms), as well as differences in the meaning of certain terms you might be more traditionally familiar with.

There are humorous comments here-and-there to keep anyone with a sense-of-humor engaged (sorry if you don't have one!) The humor is often highlighted in this manner.

This reading will repeat certain concepts to make or emphasize a point – a whole lot of material is covered. We talk about aspects of spirituality a lot, which is a word often used in many different ways, but intend to keep it simple here, and you can find our simple definition.

You will find some new angles on familiar subjects you never thought about. Thinking about things – in words – is an exercise best left to logical "thinking," but we'll mix in some emotional thinking too.

It seems some people are just sitting around waiting to be offended by something *which in itself is offensive*. If you are this-type person,

STOP READING NOW. Engage in a book-burning, even if it's only one book, burn this book NOW! Tell no-one anything so they'll have to buy their own book to burn. *To make sure you're offended, read to the end. Then you'll have to read it again so you can be doubly offended. Maybe three times is the charm.*

But it is not a goal to offend anybody, nor is it to convert or un-convert anybody to or from anything. The goal is to expose people to the truth with a capital "T," one Truth anyway, regardless of what your parents, philosophy, or religion has been trying to teach you. Someone else will be glad to give you their view, or at least refer you to a teacher that will be glad to teach their way. As Abraham tells it, there are thousands of these views. Now there are thousands plus one.

You have both *Infinity* (invisible, everything is one, and impersonal) and *Reality* (visible, everything is separate, and personal) when you are in-form, which correspond to the two sides of everyone's brain and "thinking." *Reality* has science and cookbooks, adding measurements and predictions to things once they are physical. Then we add *Life* as a referee between the invisible and visible, and is a process that takes ideas from one to the other, and back again as necessary.

If you are in-form or incarnate (or whatever other term you might want to use), you subsequently add words, logic, and reason to *Infinity* and form your *Reality*. The *Infinite* is shared, and *Reality* is personal. Remember: words are used by left-brain thinking which also uses logic and reason. Then there is *Life* that referees between them, and is very personal. Is your *Life* not personal? This has been in operation forever, but in this writing it is new.

You CAN Get There from here!

A RECAP

To get the most complete picture, read **The Way It Is**. In any event, let's recap. We'll start at the very beginning; a very good place to start. When you read you begin with A B C; when you sing you begin with Do Re Mi. So start the lyrics from the **Sound of Music** song **Do Re Mi**. It was written only 50+ years ago, but we'll NOT start at the very beginning. Of course irony rules, since *Infinity* has no beginning nor end, only eternity, but we do need some place to begin.

Beginning with *Infinity* (some call it the "G" word), you have what is non-physical, includes all possibilities, and is everywhere – there is nowhere it is not. You have, or are in *Infinity*, like it or not (we previously used "*The Infinite*.") For those wishing to identify the thinking with a specific side of the brain, it is right-brain.

Then we add the opposite, previously called "*The Finite*." (*Reality* is the same thing as *The Finite*, and comes from *Infinity*.) *Reality* occurs when you are "in-form" which is physical, everything is separate, and exists in the realm of duality (hot/cold, right/left, up/down, etc.) so we can use reason, logic, and words to talk about it. *Reality* (left-brain) "thinks" in words.

Life gets in there and acts as a referee between the invisible and the visible (*Infinity* and *Reality*). *Life* was *The Power of Creation* in **The**

Way It Is. That's the three of them, which are also the three "states" we get directly after the ho'oponopono zero state; we previously called them the *Three Pieces of Existence*.

We used to call them: *The Infinite*, *The Finite*, and *The Power of Creation*. Here we call them (invisible) *Infinity*, (visible) *Reality*, and *Life* (the referee between the invisible and visible) – they are the same things. In the current book, they are given terms which are a little more meaningful and concise, but they are the same. It is easy to match them up, 1 for 1; *after all, there's only three of them!*

The three also merge this reading with religion in an inimitable way. Christianity has the Father/Son/Holy Ghost trilogy, and the last might represent *Life*. Not being a biblical or religious scholar, it seems to fit with the three factors of *Infinity/Reality/Life*. Maybe both having three parts is just co-incidental, but there are no coincidences.

You CAN Get There from here!

WHAT'S IN A WORD?

Ephemeral is the first word I came up with for the process given here, but it did not seem to fit exactly right. According to wherever Google and Word provides definitions and synonyms, it means temporary. Does your *Life* seem temporary? Even though it technically is, sometimes it may not seem that way.

Dreamlike gets closer to the point. After all, dreams are temporary also, are they not? Good luck if you can remember a dream you had just last night, to say nothing of last week. *Dream interpretation books say they help.*

There are many explanations for dreaming, most revolving around interpretation. One explanation going off in a different direction than usual: a dream is where we "test out" different outcomes of actions before they become real. That explanation seems best.

Everything seems to share the sleep / dreaming aspect of life. Can anyone draw me a line that shows: on this side of the line one dreams; on the other side one does not dream (some humans claim to not dream ... *they don't sleep either!*)

My doGs seem to dream about chasing rabbits and squirrels judging by their legs and feet going, and barking in the back of their throat. *Maybe they are testing out what they would actually do with a school bus or motorcycle if they actually caught one!*

Some of our more poignant dreams seem to stick around longer, but try to remember most dreams tomorrow. Bet you can remember the smallest detail of some dreams years later, even if your mind is dreaming some things up. A dream may recur briefly *in one of those Deja-vu moments everyone has all over again.*

What about dreaming of getting married in June? June brides and annual baths were once the norm. Today, a person works out at a health club where showers can be taken more than once a day, but being a bride in June is still popular. *There is the phrase: "Don't throw the baby out with the bath" which most people know, but almost no-one knows where it came from, like the birds and the bush / hand saying.*

If you don't know or care if anyone has written about June brides and the bird / hand thing on Wikipedia; you are about to be enlightened about June weddings and the bathwater thing regardless, so be prepared.

Once-upon-a-time, people had an annual bath and the man went first, to be followed by the woman. Hence a wedding was in June before the soon-to-be-happy couple smelled too bad. Later came the kids, but the bathing order still started with the Father. The last bathed was the baby in, by then, dirty water. You had to take care not to "throw the baby out with the bath (water)."

I once undertook a time-study to determine how much time we spend doing anything, part of which involved determining how much time we spend in otherwise mundane activities. As it turns out, on average we spend about ½ hour a day showering, which may have included other things like brushing ones teeth and shaving. So there goes 3.5 hours, almost a half-day a week *down-the-drain.*

Besides figuring the time out, countless hours went into how to figure out said time (i.e. by spreadsheets or whatever other means used). Someone was giving advice that seemed good at the time, and this is part of it. But things keep taking forever, or almost, and this helped not one iota. See Step One for a further expansion of things taking forever, and a shift happens in Step Two. Anything you declare to be so in Step Two, you will probably get more than you wanted.

A happy medium might be desired between the smelly annual bath and a half-day a week daily shower. Maybe we have already come up with it, when *we don't shower or shave on Sundays and watch NFL all smelly and hairy* instead, so we can use the time we saved for having a clean car that week. Bathing, shower, clean, car, NFL – did you get they are all words?

The meaning of some words changes over time. Finance used to *mean* finance, which was something specific. It had to do with ratios and analysis, and accounting was its language. But it's such a cool-sounding word, evoking images of gilt and diamond encrusted mansions in the best vacation destination in the world: the "Vineyards." All the best people vacation there. Finance is now high Finance. Now, some companies no longer have an accounting department; they have a finance department because it sounds so much cooler to work in finance than in the boring accounting department. More words given by left-brain *Reality*, *Life* and logic.

The same goes for spirituality and religion. Spirituality used to mean the same as religion; but religion is boring, spirituality not-so-much. This may be because religion used to have a monopoly on everything, which includes the meaning of spirituality. Then science came along, offering to "take over now" and "New Thought Religion" sprang up offering to be the go-between. So many now use spirituality because it sounds cooler, and we can bag the implied boring religious part.

The "G" view is reinforced by Wayne Dyer telling us something a "guru" had once related to him ("guru" means closer to God): every word relating to the concept of God had the "ah" sound in it; GAHd [SIC], AHLAH [spelling intentionally changed, once again – there are two "ah"s in there!], BuddAH [the "a" and "h" are intentionally reversed], JehovAH, etc. The culture apparently doesn't matter … what counts is the word with the "ah" sound. *"Sounds" reasonable.*

Then there is "water." A limited knowledge of Spanish reveals water to be "agua," (*oh my doG, the Spanish has an AH in it!*) and they now incorporate agua in the title of some water, so you don't have to even press "2" para espanol. In the case of water, there are several different *types*: there's sparkling water, distilled water, tap water, bottled water, polluted water, toilet water (*that doGs like*) and on and on. So *we can start up the GAHd wars again and fight over the water word.*

Perrier may not even have the word for water in it, but it's branded as sparkling water for the elite, so the assigned left-brain name assures us it's NOT all the same thing. At the base, presumably all H_2O is the same anyway. *Who would fight for a couple millennia over a different word for the same thing? Those crazy humans … that's who!*

In the case of God, now there's something you can fight over, even if at the base it's all the same *Infinity*. He wasn't forcing anyone to convert to anything, because something seems wrong about (only) *say*ing you converted. One view has it the conversionator (the one forcing the conversion) doesn't really believe <whatever> anyhow, he is just trying to prove to himself he really believes it by getting someone else to say they do, too. Have you really converted to anything? *You can* say *you did.*

When I had a religion with a God, I don't think He was chopping anyone's head off if you didn't use the same word and have the same beliefs, even if "organized religion" was ultimately dropped.

There's one more reason to deep-six religion for the concept of *Infinity*. Religion says they preach Love, Forgiveness and Peace, with a super-small caveat: if you do not believe EXACTLY what they do in the EXACT same manner and use the EXACT same words at the EXACT same time, they are going to come over there and kill you. Something doesn't seem quite right about that either, so chalk that up to another reason to drop "organized religion."

In the "best practices" approach you get here, we pick and choose the best beliefs from different religions or philosophies, combine the similarities, and add things that seem logical. Every religion has good and bad points; the good points are probably why they have been around, and will stay around for a while.

A quick and easy example is in order. Catholicism is one of those religions you may need to be born into, but nothing you will find here should convince you to convert or un-convert into or out of Catholicism, or anything else.

"*Life* begins at conception" is a belief shared with Catholics, even though it currently seems to be a point of political contention. Something apparently happens after the first tri-mester to bring on *Life*; but everyone can agree that when a child is physically born, there is *Life*. One can easily see there is no need to convert anyone into or out of Catholicism, or any other form of Christianity, or any religion whatsoever.

It's really not that important to make anyone else believe your point of view where you can subsequently fight over who is RIGHT and who is WRONG for a couple millennia. Having a religion implies a single one, therefore you are: Buddhist, Jewish, Catholic, etc. and chances are good you were born into it.

If you are born (or converted) into a religion, you may then feel free to be on the "menu plan," whereby you can pick-and-choose what tenets you will follow. Such is similar to my "best practices" approach, except for the implied singularity of religion vs. the plurality approach where one gives a "thumbs-up" to the best practices.

But no-one needs to convert anyone to *Infinity*. The infinite doesn't really care if you believe it or not. No-one cares whether you think one plus one equals two either – such are mathematic principles. No-one is trying to force anyone to convert to a mathematical concept; nor have they tried to convert anyone to the belief that one plus one equals three, or tried to reverse-engineer *Infinity* so it can equal the "G" word.

Currently, the "8" lying down is accepted for *Infinity*, and we haven't made-up a different symbol or words for it. Now that it has been brought up, one can have wars over it for a couple millennia, but only if you can find a different word for *Infinity*.

CREATIONISM

Everything has consciousness, and Einstein said we cannot create nor destroy energy; can't consciousness be considered life energy, at least for humans? They are both right-brain principles anyway … simultaneously invisible, everywhere and nowhere … could they be the same thing? At the very least we can come up with a name for this branded-as-human philosophy.

Thanks to New Thought related sources and Google, "Creationism" means Creation Science, where science checks in to take over the creation dialog from religion. Science uses evolution to take-away creation from religion, and New Thought also intermediates. Realityism and Reality Science can be found on Google too, but are less popular.

Creationism has been used previously, not just in this writing; but what word hasn't already been used? It historically meant "The belief that the Universe and living organisms originate from specific acts of divine creation, as in the biblical account, rather than by natural processes such as evolution" – so says wherever Google gets its definitions. Remember: evolution is one-and-the-same-as science, at least in this work.

Supposedly there are periods in evolution that can only be explained by a divine hand taking part. How's that for bringing science and religion together? The Google definition also has belief in there, but we'll leave the religion part up to the Jehovah Witnesses coming to your door with stuff to read.

In any event, we just added another definition for Creationism, which is "The act of creating your very own visible *Reality*, along with your *Life*, from invisible *Infinity*." Don't you create your own *Reality*? Who else created it if you didn't? *Parents are fun to blame when everything seems to be going wrong!*

To make sure you can get your ISO 9001 certification, it happens like this:
1. From *Infinity*, you are given *Life* (birth) which gives you *Reality*
2. You get senses to help navigate physical *Reality*, and emotions link you back to the non-physical and otherwise invisible *Infinity*
3. Your starting beliefs are programmed by your parents or care-givers
4. *Life* brings you *Reality* as feedback, predicated on these beliefs
5. You may add (often bad) habits to your beliefs, which are always changing
6. *Life* keeps on trucking, and *Reality* gives feedback
7. You go back to the *Infinity* from which you came

It's really simple! Take the test and get the certification *so you can marry people.*

Your Mother had it right when she stated the proverbial "If everyone else is jumping off a bridge ..." What would you need to do to create your own *Reality*? To start with, do as I say. Doing as I do would be too hard to do. *LOL do-do.*

That's all there is to Creationism! Unless you stick with the basic ideals of the programming provided by your parents, society, or TV, you can change *Reality* and get new results. Such are the goals of Step One and Two: to change your *Life*!

ABOUT A DATE

There is a famous English architectural monument known to most as "Stonehenge," which was started to be built circa 3,100BC, current research and Wikipedia says. Archeologists say the stones were transferred from a quarry many miles away; no-one really knows how some of the stones are laying down on top of others, even if stones weighing several tons are secured there using one of several later-used wood methods. The site may have been used in ancient burials, but there are also some solstice and other celestial implications. It may have been used as a calendar of sorts, so people could know when to plant and harvest their crops.

We have a winter and summer solstice, which mark the shortest and longest sunlight days, respectively, and occur in Dec and Jun around the 20th thru the 22nd. Accordingly, there exists a date in the middle months (Mar, Sep) around the 20th to the 22nd in which daytime and nighttime are equal, known as the equinox.

By Dec 25th, people could superstitiously know the days would get longer again and *Life* would continue. Therefore the pagans could thank their doGs (*if they weren't already eaten*) and have a celebration. The date was used later (and still is) as the birthdate of the Savior, as part of the world switched to Christianity. Speaking of a birthdate, western scripture has descriptions of flora and fauna that do not match a winter birth, assuming other "facts" hold true.

Let us concede we create our own individual *Reality*. Do we not then choose the date and time of our "arrival?" Astrology needs a date, time, and place of birth to work, so perhaps we should have an astrologer make us a chart. Would astrology then be valid, given a date, time and place certain in which you were born? Under these assumptions, including the self-creation of *Reality*, these facts are true. Well, at least as much as you might choose them to be.

Which brings us back to a point. Have you taken someone else's advice about having an astrology chart or numerology reading done, or did you decide to do so yourself? The difference would be between an outer and inner choosing of your own beliefs, which may not be so easy to determine, so we'll let it go for now; but you might want to investigate further given the preceding information. If the idea of a chart recurs later, seemingly at random (a mark of right-brain *Infinity*), perhaps then you should have a chart done.

This is a good place to mention that you cannot plan how a certain result will come about. Planning invokes logic (as well as time), and that is NOT how *Infinity* works (it IS how logic, reasoning and the left-brain work) and plans seldom work out the way logic dictates.

Words are a necessary evil, added via left-brain logic and reason, in order to communicate how something is doing, NOT *how* it is done. Nobody knows how it gets done, that's up to *Infinity*, *Reality* and *Life*. In fact, they can accomplish two or more things simultaneously, or in conjunction with each other; the right-, left-brain and *Life* dictates how it is done. No-one knows how curing a certain ill can happen at the same time as, say, losing weight, but inquiring minds want to know and understand. If you knew how, you could sell the idea to others, who could then resell it in a qet-rich-quick scheme. *Perhaps it is better nobody knows* how *it gets done.*

Without knowing more, Astrology charts and Numerology readings communicate via words, although not specific instructions. As such, they are more like Astrology in the newspaper, or a fortune cookie, that extorts "You will have a good day." It doesn't tell you *how* to have a good day, just that you will have one.

Does *Infinity* ever speak in words? Since everything comes from *Infinity*, it must speak in words. Not only to help the left-brain "understand," but because *Reality* and *Life* both come from *Infinity*. *Understand?*

CHANGE YOUR LIFE

We all start from our single visible *Reality* we are in, like it or not. A primer is contained in this book for (invisible) *Infinity*, as well as (visible) *Reality* and *Life*, which also contains some salient points for those too impatient to do other research or other curiosity seekers. Next we remove judgment about individuals in the LOTS of consciousness entities (people) sharing our *Reality*, then go on to change locations on your very own *Roadmap-of-Life* (which intersects anyone and everyone else's roadmap in *Infinity*).

The two-halved brain pre-dated religion and politics, by a long shot, evolutionarily speaking. Graphed results support left- and right-brain "thinking," but as far as where they actually take place, who knows?

Transcendental Meditation (TM) says "equalizing" the frequencies given off by both sides of your brain is a good thing. Once a relatively small critical mass of people practicing TM occurs, it supposedly shifts the entire area in a positive direction. *Apparently contestants in the Miss World contest need to practice TM to achieve world peace.*

A popular motto of Religious Science is "Change Your Mind ... Change Your *Life*" which is consistent with New Thought. Do you have to change both sides of your brain? That would seem to require twice the effort, but changing your one mind would be easier, right?

Our pastor said replacing "wish and hope" (mental principle *keeps* you wishing and hoping) with "know and affirm" works better. Knowing and affirming will do better at releasing old beliefs, and work better than wish and hope, now that you know better. She also said once in class "If you never have another negative thought, you'll never have another negative experience."

"Well, that's easy," I thought, "I can do that!" Just drop anything resembling a negative thought, so let's start by changing your one-and-only mind. It will take less time and effort than changing both sides of your brain, logic says. *As Dr. Phil might ask, "How's that workin' out for 'ya?"*

If you ever looked at this episode of TED talks (it was among the most popular episodes), there exist two physical sides of the brain (which correspond to thinking without and with words) – the right- and the left-brain, respectively. *Infinity* and *Reality* might be another way to examine the right- and left-brain, but they might just be different modes of "thinking." Emotional / illogical is on the right, and rational / logical is on the left for right-handers. *Where thinking actually occurs, who knows, but there are definitely two physical sides to everyone's brain.*

Have you seen TED? The "T" stands for technology, the "D" for design, and the "E" – *maybe entertainment?* The TED speaker brought out to the stage what looked like a deep pizza box with somebody's brain inside, and it was attached to the spinal cord. You could actually see light between the two halves via a flashlight. *The original owner of the brain was done with it.*

No-one may be able to yet identify where the actual thinking takes place, but we *can* assign words which allude to *Infinity*. Now having words we can use to identify the two different kinds of thinking, we can understand and discuss where thinking might occur. MRIs might help identify where thinking actually takes place.

What's the difference between a logical (left-brain) and an emotional (right-brain) approach to change anyway? In the logical approach most of us use, you have chosen to do something that worked for someone else, or at least they say it worked for them when they sell it to you. Maybe you bought a program from a late-night infomercial and it worked for somebody else. Have you ever wondered why so many people try things again that don't work? There is a word that describes a person trying the same thing over and over again and expecting different results. *Hint: the word is insane.*

If the change seems to work and you have taken the logical approach, there is nothing to say it won't continue to work; your programming says whether change is possible anyway. Some philosophies have it all wrapped up in one word: worthy. Are you worthy of something better?

Your parents could have told you "You will never amount to anything" (you are unworthy) and that thought has been thought so many times over it is now a belief stored in your programming area. You *know* it to be so, and you don't even have to think about it anymore. You will die alone, unloved, and an overweight nail-biting smoker who never amounted to anything. *What about being drunk! At least you can place* that *blame on your parents; sins of the unworthy Father (you know* he *was the drunk!) who passed the belief on down.*

In the emotional approach, we start from *Infinity* where all things are possible. Starting from a specific place on your own individual *Roadmap-of-Life* – everyone is somewhere – we can consciously change our position. This should be relatively simple, especially following the included instructions. Whether a change is easy depends on what it is *and if you worthy.*

There is no way to know how this will work, depending on what the requested change is, how it is related to programming already in effect, and how pernicious any already installed programming is. This would be partially explained by the frequency the receiver's brain was in, i.e. what age were you when the programming was installed? [5]

There is one small caveat, however. You can't over-ride this change with standard thinking. Over-riding a change with traditional thinking would be the equivalent of starting in Pittsburgh (where you are), but knowing your car will never make it to Chicago (where you want to be). So you didn't check your oil, the air in your tires or anything else, since you already know you won't get there. "Knowing" is stronger than believing.

We'll start with the three *"pieces of existence"* that everyone has (*Infinity, Reality, Life*) and use spirituality, regardless of any religion or philosophy you adhere to, or don't. Whether things are visible and real, whether you believe *Reality* is of your own creation or not, it all works the same regardless, and it's really, really simple.

According to our definition of spirituality, *Infinity* (and *Life*) determines our *Reality* as well, and the Universe could care less about your definitions or any philosophy. We all have spirituality with its three components, like it or not.

BTW (By-the-Way, for old folks), religion is just a philosophy of living, maybe with some rules carved on stone tablets for good order, followed by a certain number of people. Some religions get some politics and law stirred in for added enforcement, like we in America have. One source had 4,000 religions in existence, some use other numbers. Some people even *say* they follow a specific religion. The word "say" is emphasized because, well, *words are cheap!*

Ideas are just one way *Life* determines whether something should be checked-back-in to *Infinity* from *Reality*, so *Life* is like a celestial librarian. This or that particular idea is simply an idea not yet finding its time. Didn't someone once say something about an "idea that has found it's time?"

This example is given in **_The Seth Material_**, where Seth asks if Jane's husband, Robert, remembers being one of two brothers at an early point in his life, and of course there is their mother. Seth continues by saying there are actually three creations of the mother, one by each of the brothers, as well as one by the mother herself. How can that be?

Therein lies the difference: the majority of people would believe the mother is an independent creation who is merely observed by the brothers (as well as the mother herself, especially if she were to look in the mirror) however they learned to do so. A very slim minority can be said to use the three separate creations aspect, each created independently, described here.

In the case of the observer, the brothers have beliefs in which they have been told or educated to think in that way, especially by society, or they just picked it up. They are behaving in the way society or culture says they "should."

In the case where everyone creates their own *Reality*, the brothers (and the mother herself) have the belief they came up with their creations separately, independently, and by themselves. Like learning how to look, no-one told or taught them how. They are NOT behaving in a manner society or culture says they "should."

The belief about the mother and her sons was accordingly programmed, but do you get the difference?

The observers have their beliefs and *Life* coming at them from the outside, and they have little or nothing to do with the creation of their *Reality*. The exception would be their beliefs, which are always internal.

The remaining small minority make their own beliefs and individual *Reality* from the inside. Actually, your internal beliefs create your *Reality*, and it is how your beliefs get there that matters.

How could the brothers each create a separate (but almost equal) mother if they did not also create completely separate *Realities* from separate beliefs? As previously mentioned, it all works the same, so who cares? But they are completely opposite methods of belief creation, and DO NOT yield the same outcomes, even if both methods seem to yield the same results. Remember: they are just your own beliefs, aren't they?

The minority use the exact opposite when forming their beliefs, to what the majority know how to do and is doing (the word "know" is added tongue-in-cheek). "Unanswered Questions in Life 101" didn't teach me what to do either, although I have the certificate somewhere. *Why does the water go up-and-down in your toilet on a windy day? 101 did not give me an answer to* that *unanswered question either.*

While the child is being programmed (and throughout his *Life*), most parents unconditionally love their children no matter what the child or children do (*in which case the parent might be said to be more akin to a doG*), while some just don't … others are in-between. We'll also forget about the person going to their therapist who has a friend that has the parents who … and get back to the person interested in changing their own *Life. But parents are so much fun to blame for all those things that have NOT gone RIGHT!*

35

Before we begin changing anyone's *Life*, let's think a minute. Most recently there is politics; some forms of politics seek to disavow any religion at all. *The political leaders are just lawyers who will believe anything for a buck.*

Then there was America and all that implies, which some would say includes Judea-Christian religion. There were Ten Commandments in the Judea-Christian Religion, and Ten Amendments in American politics in the bill-of-rights. Ten is an easy number to remember, and apparently is a good number for both religion and politics.

If we cancelled BOTH ten AND thirteen, would doing so cancel out both politics AND religion, as well as high-rise buildings and hotels now having neither a tenth nor thirteenth floor? Perhaps a person should specifically book a hotel stay on the tenth or thirteenth floor just to prove they have no politics or religion.

Some people will actually read this material with the goal of changing their *Life*. Most won't even acquire it, but if they do, chances are good it's on their shelf or bookstand in the "to be read" area. Those that never read this book might feel their *Life* is already hunky-dory, or there is nothing they can do about it anyway – they are in the majority of people.

There are two types of readers of this material. The first type reads everything they can get their hands on regarding spirituality, and might be academics or curiosity seekers, including those who want to see how this worked for others. Reading this book would at least make you feel like an academic if you are so inclined. Maybe they'll try it out later, and just dip their toe in now, and see how it worked for others.

Why would anyone read anything about changing something you already feel good about, or can't do anything about? Some might read in order to feel superior to others, but there are those who feel they *can* change things, or might read this anyway.

The second type of reader wants to actually do the work to make procedures detailed within happen for them. The person that wants to change will eventually encompass members from either group, and members of a group will shift as a curiosity seeker decides he or she really wants to change their *Life*.

Those that start off wanting actual change in their *Life*, later decide it requires too much time-and-effort. It's so much easier to simply learn about others, or take a certain color of pill somebody else pays for. *If it is the weekend, a blue pill might be in order.*

Those who started by dipping in their toe are ready to take the plunge; others that plunged right in want to get out, dry off, and take a change pill. *A change pill would normally have a certain color (probably* NOT *blue) and the side-effects would include "unusual dreams."*

The people wanting real change have woken up at some point in their *Life* NOT liking where they are, and want to exist somewhere different. They may not like the politics, their financial situation, or health to name a few "problem areas."

Of course, there are some philosophies that state concentrating on what is *wrong* will get you more of the same, but here we only seek to acknowledge the problems to find your place on the map. The fully awake-and-aware person knows they are *responsible* for exactly where they are, even if they don't know – or care – how they got there.

Everyone got exactly where they are as the end result of all the choices they made. The choices were served up via your place on the roadmap at the time. Then you (nobody else) made the choice. You can even remember all your decisions if you try hard enough. Right now, however, you want to start making choices which get you onto a different location on your *Roadmap-of-Life*. So what is it that is supposed to happen?

It was not long ago people were tried as heretics (*gotta' love them religions!*) when they dared espouse the theory the earth was *NOT* the center of everything. Shortly thereafter our galaxy was the only one there was. Now our *Reality* is the only one there is, but we are quickly learning differently. Just remember, there are still "flat earthers" out there, and most people in existence are "flat *Reality*ers." An analogy has been developed by which a standard 2D Roadmap, which can be acquired at any gas station, is transformed into many dimensions for use as a tool for examining your *Life*. A roadmap, starting out flat, might help bridge the gap between flatness and multi-dimensional *Reality*.

A 2D Roadmap might be rudimentary, because your *Life* resembles something with more than two dimensions. The Akashic Records, resembling this multi-dimensional roadmap, was popular with Theosophists around the time of the founding of this country. Multi-dimensional roadmaps are still useful, because something similar is tapped into by "readers" (card readers, numerology readers and astrology-chart preparers, or other people that claim to have knowledge of your future by seeing where you are today) even if the source is complex or even infinite. You are always somewhere on some page of your *Roadmap-of-Life*, and headed somewhere else. *If you're not somewhere on some roadmap, how does that happen?*

According to the New York state tourist bureau, there is so much to see in NY, you need never leave the state. According to statistics, a lot of people never go beyond a relatively limited birth area. Some go, some don't, some never get a roadmap. That's just *Life*.

After you refer to your *Roadmap-of-Life*, you might then use your roadmap to get from point A to point B in *Life* – in this instance point B is someplace better you have specifically chosen. To get to point B, you have to go beyond birth, programming, and bad habits; such is a goal of changing your place on your very own *Roadmap-of-Life*. *You're not stuck with your programming, no matter how it seems!*

You CAN Get There from here!

CONSCIOUSNESS ENTITIES

The term "consciousness entity" describes an entity that has consciousness, and as such it can be with or without form. In our one-and-only *Reality*, we have LOTS of consciousness entities floating around (or whatever they do) when not in form. When one is physical, he or she is known to be in-body or incarnate, and accordingly has a *Reality* and *Life*.

Seth (a dis-incarnate consciousness entity channeled by Jane Roberts) says the entities are having a blast in-between lives deciding who will be whom (father, mother, sibling, etc.) in their next *Reality*. Seth often talks about those consciousness entities we would classify as human and visible, but in-between lives is a hoot. The Law of Attraction (LOA) says much the same thing, and living a happy life when one is in it. The LOA addresses consciousness entities between lives, because it is, well, a channeled work FROM these entities.

Seth also says consciousness entities will adopt a form when they have decided who will play whom, in order to learn whatever "lessons" that are available, although nothing is "carved in stone." Some consciousness entities will decide to re-incarnate later, to learn whatever lessons might be learned then. The majority of consciousness entities will do so in the future in our terms, if at all. Remember: *Infinity* has no time, so later or in the future is of no real relevance.

Nothing further was found about what said lessons might be, so there may be too many of them, or maybe they are too specific to an individual to note – maybe both. Developing the explanation given here, as well as becoming an author might be among *my* lessons.

Most of us cannot communicate with the not-in-body "others," and accordingly will start (and stay) in the single *Reality* we are used to. Some claim to be guided by "angels," and these may be not-in-form humans – Christianity has angels. Our hubris would have us believe since we are the only ones with ("I think, therefore I am") what we can identify as consciousness, we might think we are the only ones coming and going from physical form.

A birds-and-the-bees talk. Before you get all freaked out like it is one of your parents talking to you, it's not. "Birds-and-the-bees" are pets narrowed down to just pets like doGs; current research shows doGs have 300 to 700 times the smelling power of humans (smelling lights up a whole area of their brain on doggie MRIs), but you will never see them stopping to smell the roses, because more interesting smells abound. The following discussion might comfort some who would like the persistence of their pet's consciousness.

As far as we know, doGs get the same physical senses we do – sight, sound, smell, taste, and touch. Since they have no literal left- and right-brains, interpretation of senses may or may not be involved. DoGs may or may not get emotions also, and people have varying thoughts about this. They learn to use their senses, only faster. Some senses, like smell, they seem to get more out of. Sight may require doGs looking directly at something to perceive motion.

Horses have way bigger noses than a doG, and the word is they can smell water way off, but maybe it's something else we only attribute to smell. Polar Bears supposedly have the keenest sense of smell of all animals, and if you want to get close enough to compare the size of a horse's nose to a polar bear's nose, you can measure them both. Personally, I'd rather be closer to any kind of a horse than a polar bear. A further discussion of nose size and senses, including smell, is not included.

Since they're closest to us, our pets take on special roles as consciousness entities, including those that wind up physically closest to us: doGs, cats, and horses, etc. Some people even have reptiles as pets. They may have noses, but snakes are supposed to "smell" with their tongue! I don't know, nor do I really care or will ever find out, how they come to be here in the physical with us.

DoGs have been known to make it "home" over extraordinary distances, and butterflies migrate back to the same place over long distances and generations. How they do this is a subject for extensive scientific research, and not covered here.

If we create our own *Reality*, this implies we create our pets along with everything else, but maybe *Infinity* acts differently. Cats are pretty independent and seem to get here on their own. *Like the woman in the sitcom says: "Do I have to go to the animal shelter, or do they arrive automatically?"*

Who knows about other consciousnesses they may have, along with different sorts we would not recognize, like the consciousness of rocks and trees. There may be a tree that recognizes a person that passes it every day. *Ask it.* Perhaps we create them, or we just move into an area already occupied by them, given our co-creation. There is one key: co-creation, but we will not get into co-creation either!

Let's start with an incarnate (in-body) example for humans. Forget all the views about choosing to be here, your parents and *Life*, etc. You might sum it up by saying something about lessons to learn, etc.

but maybe you have nothing to say about it, like going to cosmic school.

We will proceed with something most would agree you have no control over: your height. Short, tall, average; you never chose it. *Why would anyone – even most females – choose to be short in our culture?* That would give us three possibilities.

Then add weight, which some argue you have some control over: skinny, fat, average. That adds three more to a matrix that now has nine potentials, one of which would be tall and skinny. *Some of us should be so "lucky!" It's better than being short-and-fat.*

Also forget about changes that might happen over time, like your weight. Let's consider time to be static, like the point-in-time when you are thirty years old, after you have lost the excess baby-weight, should you ever lose it! The kids are off to school.

The important point is: you are now in a matrix of nine cells, which we'll call "options" from the perspective of the matrix. It is not hard to imagine with the expansion of a few more options, the matrix would become very large.

Add the liberal or conservative option, along with those calling themselves one-or-the-other (or neither), into the mix. As far as liberal or conservative goes, our side is smart, the other side is just plain stupid. *If you add how often one drops the "F-bomb" to prove how smart they are, you will probably get the F-N idea.*

Do you really think you are going to convince the other side to change their view, from liberal to conservative or vice-versa? You would be just as successful convincing a tall person they are really short. Of course, you could always do that by convincing the NBA to take a 6-foot-five person and make him feel like he was five-foot-two. *That might take changing basket heights.*

You get the idea: changing a person from liberal to conservative or vice-versa would probably not work out well. Nor would changing most of their other characteristics, and there's a lot. A LOT of options are available in the incarnate matrix, regardless of how popular any "slot" might be, and that's before you add-in different cultures.

There are many, many cells available in the matrix, and the matrix is for only those who are on the planet and visible right now; everyone ultimately gets their own cells in their own matrix. But that's all logical stuff with words, and we will get to judgment soon enough.

As one goes from the visible to the invisible, one also switches from LOTS to a possible infinite number of potential consciousnesses (also LOTS) going from (visible) *Reality* to the (invisible) *Infinite*. LOTS serve both: in the visible world, it is 6-8 Billion (LOTS); in the invisible it is just LOTS.

Consciousness entities may sit around *Infinity* having a hoot figuring out who will play what role in the next reincarnation, but we have forgotten about that for now. Also remember (*er, forget*) next has no meaning for *Infinity*; all incarnations / re-incarnations might be simultaneous there.

WTF (*figure* that *out!*)

CHRISTIANITY

If there were only someone in Christianity who could explain what the Holy Ghost / Spirit thing is, along with the cross symbol on their chest Catholics do with their upright hand. I've tried kneeling and have given up. *Forgive them Father for they know not what they do. At least the "kneelers" are padded!*

I AM well over waiting for someone to explain the third aspect of the Christianity trio: the Holy Ghost (or Spirit) part. I forgot to ask about it in my last discussion with Jehovah's Witnesses. I might be correct in analyzing this third part must be *Life*, since Father and Son seem to fit nicely with *Infinity* and *Reality*, at least once I added free thinking into the mix.

There is a passage in Hebrews 11 that says something about what you see not coming from what you see. To say it another way, the visible comes from the invisible, and refers to *Reality* coming from *Infinity*. You can find out more specifics about the passage when a Jehovah's Witness comes to your door. To become a Jehovah Witness, you are required to know where the passage, quote, or verse comes from in the bible they carry. *Try it out – say nothing about Hebrews 11, and see if a Jehovah Witness can come up with it!*

We celebrate Dec 25 as the birthday of Christ, with all that implies: Black Friday, presents for kids, and Department Stores, etc. The date was chosen in an effort to sustain traditions that revolved around the winter solstice. Celebrating Christ's birthday would be the same as celebrating your greatest math teacher's birthday, say May 20th, and not the fact he taught you one plus one equals two.

It is strange that Christianity's holiest day, celebrating the Resurrection of Christ, is Easter. Even though it is a holiday, it contains none of Dec 25th hoopla, and contains almost nothing but rabbits, eggs, and shoes!

The New Testament, which is supposed to be all about Christianity, was not even written until some 300 years after the "death" of Christ during the Council of Nicea. Supposedly there are scriptural references to spring flowers occurring around the same time as the birth of Christ, the "immaculate conception," etc.

There is an eMail joke about someone leaving out a letter (before the printing press was invented) upon copying scripture, which is why Catholic Priests are celebate. The world is supposed to celebrate the birth of Christ. Celebrate contains an "r." Oops!

I still find lyrics and tunes from popular Christian Holiday classics running around my brain during Holiday time. I can only assume I was programmed with these at a very-early age, before any conscious recall at a later date. Even though many are secular having to do with "Santa," many are decidedly Christian, like **We Three Kings**. Maybe some songs came from **The Simpsons** because the lyrics I AM thinking of: "*We Three Kings of Orient Are … Smoking on a Rubber Cigar*."

Anything having to do with any form of Christian religion is about *Life*. Throw in some commandments (rules carved in stone) about behaving, and you have a one-stop-shop for how to live. Just be careful not to covet, says religion. "That's easy," you are thinking.

Now it's *my* wife, not my brother's, and I don't even have a brother. Of course, you might also get a mortgage and car payments, *but those are just details where the Devil must be lurking.*

Remember the religious commandment about not coveting something your brother has? Better to spend your mental energy on getting your own houses, boats, and jets, to say nothing of getting a wife or losing weight.

Programs you can purchase are supposed to help you lose weight or stop smoking, and both are logical procedures. Things about *Reality* have been misconstrued; the same happens to *Life*, and both are left-brain. *Reality* and *Life* just happen, there is nothing you can do about it, and the *WRONG* construction would be it is not individually formed. Relax and stop trying to convince others of how *RIGHT* you are, which also includes judging them as *WRONG*.

As far as laying claims to be a biblical scholar goes, I *do* accept the "red letter Bible." The passages in red, although limited in number, are supposedly directly attributable to Christ, as truths spoken by one of the great mystics. Remember: it is not my objective to convert anyone into or out of anything religious, because there are many mystics out there, and they have many words of truth for us.

Let us concern ourselves with some of the letters in red, which supposedly Christ said:

1. Ask NOT what your Country can do for you *(sorry, that was JFK, who was decidedly un-Christ-like depending on who you ask)*
2. These things that I do, you can do better *(which prompted me to write the song* Anything I Can Do You Can Do Better *sung to the tune of* Anything You Can Do I Can Do Better*)* which was uttered by Christ, predicated on the usage of the "I" pronoun and

3. It is done to you as you believe (*"to" replaced "unto," and "ye" was replaced by "you" here*).

There seems to be a need to be a label attached to *<whatever>*, so people can identify with and understand it. The label is, of course, a word (words are some of the things the left-brain uses while "thinking" about a subject). Even though it may have taken a while to assign the label of "Christianity" to the teachings of Jesus Christ, Christianity remains popular with followers in the western world some 2,000 years later.

Christianity has a lot going for it. I speak from the experience of having spent the most time in Christianity with the exception of New Thought, especially in childhood where I was programmed, even if I rejected Christianity later.

Christianity gives us the idea of a soul, but "free thinking" (and Abraham) provides that some part of the consciousness entity always remains in invisible *Infinity*, whether the consciousness entity is physical or not. Free thinking parts with Christianity here, since the Christian soul apparently parks for an eternity (a really, really long time) once it is freed from its "earthly bonds" and goes to heaven (*or pushes the big <DOWN> button in the afterLife elevator*).

BTW, my left-brain "understanding" is: up and down used to be reversed. When you pressed the <DOWN> button in your elevator-of-life, you would be headed toward a heaven contained *within* the earth, and not the opposite. So push the <DOWN> button and see where it leads.

Not being a bigot, everybody else seems to love to hate Jews and blacks. It doesn't have anything to do with religion, does it? Jews are probably born into the Jewish religion, and inordinately stay that way. Blacks seem to follow Christianity or Islam, but the ratio is unknown (Islam is the most popular western religion elsewhere). Christianity is said to be the most popular western religion, at least in America and Europe.

So much for Christianity having some things *RIGHT,* but other things *WRONG.* Judgment about what stories are *RIGHT,* and which is *WRONG* is not included here. Let's have a war between religions, which is so much better than a war between two sects of the *SAME RELIGION. But all wars are great, aren't they?*

You CAN Get There from here!

ONE IS THE LONELIEST NUMBER

Suppose it is now one second, one minute, one hour or one whatever since you have died – PLUS now you're dead. Have you noticed they always start the NEWS off noting how many people died doing <whatever>? So death is given to be important to our western culture.

Death would be a really, really long dirt-nap; looking at grass growing from the other side; take a swim wearing cement overshoes, are a couple euphemisms. "A couple" indicates more than one, and there are many euphemisms for death.

We might tell how important something is by the number of euphemisms. Besides being dead, you might be really lonely. But don't worry, there's more one's involved so you needn't be lonely, and you're never really lonely anyway.

> *One is the loneliest number that you'll ever do*; *Two can be as bad as one*
> *It's the loneliest number since the number one*
> **Three Dog Night; *One***

One may be the loneliest number, but apparently it's worse than two, or just as bad. One is the number often representing Unity in mathematics, so it would seem Unity is lonely too. Two would probably be male and female, so we'll just go back to One. *At least One is just lonely.*

Zero times anything is zero. It doesn't matter how large or small anything is. When you multiply it by zero, you get zero. But every rule has an exception, and this rule is no exception. Zero times infinity is one, and one is unity. These may be mathematical – slash – spiritual definitions, and mathematics is said to approximate *Reality*, but the Spiritual *IS Reality*!

Death becomes you. Wasn't that a line in a book or movie? Should you ever become lonely, just remember death where you are never lonely. Just remember all the consciousness entities which surround you when you're invisible. There is more than One … LOTS of them.

Also keeping it simple, there are no parents, kids, pets or other heirs and assigns in the picture. A $1MM figure is floating around (that's one million dollars). On the one hand, the $1MM is positive (that's $1MM in assets); on the other hand, the $1MM is negative (that's a $1MM debt owed to one or more people). *I told you there were more un-lonely ones!*

After you have passed on, do you really think you care which one it is: asset or debt? If it was a positive million dollars, did you really think you could take it with you? If you thought you were going to leave it to your kids, ask the Government. If it were a negative million dollars, do you really think some eternal bill collector is going to be following you around, calling at inconvenient times? *How much more inconvenient can it be than if you're dead – the ultimate inconvenience?*

Being dead is even more inconvenient than bill collectors calling when you're on the throne or eating dinner! *All bills are excused, unless you've left your estate to a relative, then they're inconvenienced for a while.*

Have you ever wondered how someone "has it all," while those starting in similar circumstances have nothing? At the same time, some of those having it all are miserable and some of those with nothing are happy. How does *that* happen? A cultural norm has us all running around happily judging people on how many things or how much money they have.

We'll start off in the single *Reality* we all know and love, despite there being ample proof of multiple *Realities*. It wasn't that long ago we were all "flat earthers." Now flat earthers is a political term, but we're all "single *Reality*ers" right now.

Maybe you're lonely. But we start off being an un-lonely one among LOTS of consciousness entities. Since you are reading this in the physical, you have chosen to be a consciousness entity who is also physical right now.

We all start off from *Infinity* where we are all consciousness entities when you are NOT physical. There's LOTS of consciousness entities, and that's why you're NOT lonely, especially when you're NOT physical.

Before we go any farther, let's explore the source of the very first term coined, and its usages, that help explain spirituality. "*Piece of Existence*" is the term, and *Infinity*, *Reality*, and *Life* explain the details we are all stuck with. Father, Son, and Holy Ghost come from Christianity, then we add in some features from New Thought Religion, and free thinking completes it.

Free thinking also gives us the person who physically represents consciousness, and gets reeled back in to *Infinity* once *Reality* and *Life* have fulfilled their pact. The consciousness entity becomes formless once again and is thereby back in *Infinity*.

Infinity, *Reality*, and *Life* just might be different parts of the same thing, because they all come from *Infinity*. You are a person, which helps close the circle between *Infinity* and *Life* (the invisible impersonal and visible personal).

Reality and *Life* get personalized as they become individual, and you can thereby identify with them as an individual. *Infinity*, in total, contains all the consciousnesses you could want, hence becoming a singular consciousness entity makes the entity personal.

With a lot of help from Channeled sources, free thinking completes what happens when consciousness decides to become real and appear again "in person", to learn whatever "lessons" are available now, but no lesson is "carved in stone."

Free thinking also provides an impetus that helps explain how you form your own *Reality*, courtesy of an offhand comment made by Seth in ***The Seth Material*** regarding a mother and her two sons. Seth notes that there are actually three creations of the mother figure via the two young siblings, and herself. How can that be?

There are also all these *Realities* – LOTS of them – which will accommodate LOTS of creations. But we'll also keep *Reality* and *Creation* singular for now. Probably your grandparents, and maybe your parents, have chosen to move beyond the merely physical. In any event, 100 years ago, and in 100 years hence, none of you was or will be physical. Such is my 100-Year rule.

The only thing that is permanent and unchanging is that which already has everything – *Infinity*. Despite having your face carved on Mt. Rushmore, nothing physical is permanent. See whose face is left on any monument after the next ice age *if you're still around.*

Einstein says energy can neither be created nor destroyed, but can only change form. What did he know, anyway? *Despite his cute little "e=mc²" equation, he helped invent the atom bomb. But what's one little mistake?*

Einstein chose to be in our "little" (finite) brain for a while, even if his face was not carved onto any mountain, *but* his hair was transferred to Don King. At least we all now have "free" power. Nixon learned marketing well and used the "free" word.

Many have chosen to be here for a while, and now they're not, which is why I call those physically here a "minority," even though they may be large in number. What's the population of our planet now? 6, 7, or 8 billion, *despite those who think people should number no more than 60 thousand.*

What's the number of invisible consciousness entities in the "majority"? LOTS. Those consciousness entities who have chosen NOT to be here right now, are probably larger in number, hence they are in the "majority." Who's in the visible "minority?" LOTS.

Many call communications with those of us not physically here "talking with Angels," so we can also include the Angels of Christianity. Remember: anything and everything is possible in the *Infinity* which contains all possibilities, including majorities and minorities of consciousness entities.

Many will find solace about pets who have passed on might also be consciousness entities, to be contacted in the great beyond (as are the squirrels and rabbits doGs love to chase, along with anything having any sort of consciousness, which occupy our great outdoors consciousness entities). Trees and rocks are supposed to have consciousness too, but of a kind we would never recognize. But we'll keep our hubris under control while constraining consideration to the human brand of consciousness entity, and thus keep things less complicated in our discussion.

You are right here in our single *Reality*, reading this using one or more senses you were born with as you become physical. You probably don't remember how or why you got sight, sound, smell, taste or touch, but you learned how to use them in your first few years to get around in our physical *Reality*. You may have learned to "look both ways before crossing" but that is an added-on rule; no-one taught you how to look.

In our western culture, you probably never learned how to use emotions *at all*, especially not to communicate with your "significant other" (LOL) who remains in non-physical *Infinity*. Your significant other remains in *Infinity*.

If you are male, you're allowed by society to exhibit emotion (anger or joy) when "our team" loses or wins, even if you have never been to "our city." The players claim to represent the city *if they are paid enough*, but may never have been to our city.

This is especially true if you are in a sports bar and have had a couple shots, but don't ever cry over losing! NEVER show any emotion, except for a high-five of joy when our team scores or wins. Fortunately for women, you are emotionally a little less up-tight. Just don't cry if our team loses – it's unseemly! *A man is allowed a tiny smidgen of emotion (grief) if his doG dies, but that's very temporary.*

No-one can tell us *how* we produce our *Reality* movie from our consciousness, but we can speculate as to *why*. Speculation has it we will experience our thinking, mostly unconscious, as "real" when our *Reality* reflects what we are thinking. Chances are it doesn't feel all that good if someone else or something (like your parents, society, or a TV infomercial) wrote or directed your movie. It doesn't matter if someone told us to think that way, or whether we came up with the movie ourselves; the results are the same.

Either way, we get the results of what we are thinking, have been programmed to do, or we might simply be stuck in a habit. Our beliefs going on inside have become "real" to us on the outside. Here's a hint: everything – that's *everything* – going on in the movie of our *Reality* is a result of our beliefs. Don't know what you think (and believe), consciously or not? Just look around.

Everyone is someplace on your very own *Roadmap-of-Life*. If you're NOT somewhere, tell me how that happened! You can consciously change to someplace else, or just take your hands off the wheel and see where *Life* leads. Even taking your hands off the wheel is a choice.

Either way you're going to be somewhere else; the difference is whether you have chosen to be there, or have just let *Life* go on by default. In 100 years neither you nor the Universe is going to care anyway – such is the 100-Year rule.

The Universe knows nothing about what you may or may not want, whether it's good or bad (human value judgments can change person-to-person), or how much or little you may correspondingly want of it. It only knows what you are concentrating on, and gives you more of it so you can know you are on *that* track. The Universe could care less about whatever-it-is you have judged "bad" and may want less of. Remember: what is "good" to some is "bad" to others, including MONEY.

The Judea-Christian "golden rule" states "do unto others, as you would have them do unto you" which is also an internal belief. Remember the old Christian adage "You get what you believe?" I may have given up Christianity too soon. Then again, maybe not.

You CAN Get There from here!

THE ROADMAP

A 2D Roadmap may be useful to know where you are, but it is not useful to know how you got there (unless you wish to know all the wrong turns you made, but that would be looking backward, as in the wake is still steering the boat).

There must be people who look at the map and wonder where they made a wrong turn, but that is not the object here. But if you want to go to Chicago, it is useful to know if you are already in Pittsburgh or San Diego.

You should not care how you got to be here (such would be looking backwards, which also includes the whole pillar of salt thing, according to Judea-Christian philosophy). At the very least, moving forward, you would want to know if you want to go East or West. Maybe you want to go South or North to see other sights along the way, but that's a whole 'nother story.

At a bookstore, you might acquire a spiral-bound book containing a map for every state. It doesn't matter if the book does not contain maps for Europe, it still exists (*take our word for it*) even if you never go there – the same for any state like Hawaii. You may never go to Hawaii, but it still exists and may even have a page-or-two in the spiral-bound book to prove it. It may only have maps for the two largest islands and cities, but the other islands are still there. You'll have to take our word that they're still there, *unless you visit and take the tour.*

Speaking of Hawaii, I will relate an opening joke read by *The Car Guys* on NPR. *Cars are male, of the lonely one variety, regardless of car shows on TV starring females.* I think the man in the joke must have started out in San Diego. Nobody cares how he got there.

> *A guy is walking down the beach and he finds a bottle. He rubs it and out pops a Genie who will grant him a wish, but one wish only.*
>
> *After thinking a while, the fellow says he always wanted to visit Hawaii, but if he goes there he would be stuck, because he is afraid of flying, gets seasick, and couldn't get back.*
>
> *"I know" he exclaims! "Build me a bridge and I can drive there and back!" he orders the Genie.*
>
> *The Genie thinks for a moment and asks if the person knows what he is asking. "I would have to go over or under the shipping lanes like the Chesapeake Bay Bridge-Tunnel, and build pilings and footings several thousand feet deep to the bottom of the ocean. Is there anything else you might want?"*
>
> *The man thinks for a moment, then asks "Can you explain to me the mind of a woman?"*
>
> *The Genie asks "Will that be two or four lanes?"*
>
> *Lighten up ladies – it's just a joke ! ! !*

Although it is useful to know whether you are currently in Pittsburgh or San Diego, it is not important to know how you got there. You can safely assume you have more strong than weak points, or else you probably wouldn't be visible on the planet reading this and making an attempt to change your *Life*. YOU ARE NOW STEERING the boat, and the wake is done steering.

You can come at changing your *Reality* from a couple different directions. You might very well think "Well, since I HAVE a *Reality*, by the definition given here (and logic) I must also have a *Life*, so all I need to do is select where I would like to be, and keep feeling good." It's all details, *and the Devil is hiding in there somewhere!*

Starting with a left-brain logical approach, you would be using a program set forth by someone else. Such left-brainism might be behavior originally programmed into you by your parents, since you need to have someone to blame when you don't succeed! But there is an important difference: when you follow something set forth by someone else, it supposedly worked for at least (or *only*) one other person – them! It's much more fun to keep trying different things anyway.

They sell their approach to you, and it's supposed to work the same for you. Just follow the program explicitly (with their 60-day money-back guarantee) and your *Life* will be completely transformed, and you FINALLY will be done with smoking or overeating. How can you go wrong in 60 days? It may indeed work (or not) and you've got a whole 60 days to transform your life anyway.

If your life is not transformed, you can always purchase somebody else's plan and try that. Some people purchase every left-brain program offered that also includes a money-back guarantee, just so they can say it didn't work and get their money back without even trying it. Why would anyone do that?

Changing your *Reality* is entirely possible via only a logical left-brain "from the outside" approach. You might first choose from what seems like an infinity of choices, and afterward you can purchase a program guaranteed to help you stop smoking or lose weight in a left-brain manner.

Feeling good brings in emotion and its resultant communication with the great beyond – right-brain thinking (this is consistent with what is taught by the Law of Attraction). When you include feeling good, you must be using both your logical left-brain along with the creative right.

Another way is the right-brain approach, starting from the invisible *Infinity* where everything is possible. Start from where you are right now on your very own *Roadmap-of-Life*, then change your location. Also, getting your beliefs "from the inside" corresponds to an aspect of your own creation.

Where you want to be is just another possibility from an infinite range of possibilities – it is no more complicated than that. Infinite possibilities will bring something forward no matter how illogical, and the left-brain will complete it via logic. We will use the techniques found here to change your location on your *Roadmap-of-Life*. Feeling good is a side-effect of emotion, which does not require the FDA to approve.

The "from the inside," or right-brain emotional approach to creating your *Reality* (given in this book) uses *your own details* to effect a change, and would normally include no words. Yes, the plan might be provided by someone else and use words to communicate it, but it uses *details* set out on your *very own Roadmap-of-Life* – such is the difference.

This is not to say there are not some wonderful "programs" out there, but while they may have worked for someone else, the ones that keep working tend to be more generic and cost little or nothing. Having gratitude is a good example.

You cannot be both grateful, and hold anything else in mind, someone once said. Keep being grateful regardless, if you are on the generic grateful program. You might be grateful for stopping smoking, but the specific program was designed by, and worked for, someone else.

You probably purchased some patch or program to stop smoking, and now that it has worked, you are grateful – for a while at least. Look out after you have dropped the gratitude. Just remember, there are many others who have temporarily stopped smoking via one of several methods and are not grateful, and have started smoking again.

The first way, heretofore used by mostly everyone, would have you following a plan set forth by someone else. They rolled out a red, blue, grey (color is not important) carpet for you to follow, and there is usually a monetary price involved in the transaction. The program provider would get the money, less of course, what is paid to anyone else involved in selling it to you over the phone at dinnertime.

Making sense of something, or figuring something out, is the way logic and reason work. Follow the model set forth by someone else to follow logic and reason. Since you already have a *Reality* dictated by *Life*, it would seem following a plan set out by someone else would be difficult, keep you working, and ultimately choosing and buying another plan.

A second way (our way) is to have you change your place on your very own *Roadmap-of-Life* which is totally your creation, and there is no MONEY involved. There is nothing to say that changing your place by purchasing a patch / program to help you get to a place of non-smoker won't work. Actually there is one reason. You have just received a hint, but can you figure it out? Oops, there's another hint.

The right-brain will present alternatives that might make no sense whatsoever to the left-brain, so just do it, even if it doesn't make sense. But each alternative will work regardless, especially if you do not follow one-after-the-other. Such would be the left-brain talking using logical thinking which includes linear time. Speaking of linear time, results might occur simultaneously, but which one actually worked? Could it be both of them worked?

If you want to stop drinking, first join AA, then get with the 12 steps and become a friend of Bills'. Notice "then" (as well as the 12 steps which are supposed to be performed one-after-the-other) indicates linear time. You, too, could become a dry-drunk and be addicted to going to meetings, before you fall off the wagon and get drunk again right after a meeting, *OR* you could change your place on your very-own *Roadmap-of-Life*.

In the story part of both Step One and Step Two, naming them something simple helps. For Step One, the simple name is to acknowledge where you are (before). Step Two would name where you want to be (after). As we have said, the label is necessary only for communication – NOT to make this process left-brain. When your *Life* is created by you, everything falls into place.

If you want to lose weight, you could take the left-brain approach and join Weight Watchers, reason (and their ad) tells you. But watch out. If you *say* you are tired of being overweight, you can be overweight AND tired. It's better to set a specific poundage, acknowledge where you are, then know and affirm you are NOT tired.

There is one little requirement: you need to choose and name where you want to be on your *Roadmap-of-Life*. Choosing a different location would be something akin to: I know and affirm I AM a healthy, non-smoking person with lots of energy. Keep it simple.

Something taught in Science of Mind is "Know and Affirm," because it works much better than hope or wish, which, according to mental principle will keep you hoping and wishing. There you have it: both are mental principles. Are you "tired" of being overweight?

You CAN Get There from here!

ALREADY TRUE

What most would consider "normal" thoughts are left-brain, where your thought involves words and take reason, logic and time. Time is another offshoot of rational thinking. Look how much around you already reflects what you believe and think, consciously or unconsciously. *Hint: it all does.*

Remember: a belief is a thought that is thought so many times it eventually becomes a conscious thought no more, and is pushed down into the sub-conscious where it operates below the level of normal awareness. A belief is inside you, and is much easier once you don't have to think about it, and it has thereby been programmed. The source of the belief is indeterminate. The belief can ultimately come from the outside or the inside.

Programming at an early age may include "bad" items, but so are some habits picked up later. Regardless of what one or both parents programmed into you, it's still fun to blame them when things don't go right. I know they had good intentions, but there's a road somewhere paved with them.

Blaming your parents, or anyone else, is *so much fun*. You are programmed by your parents or caregivers early on, and their otherwise free advice is worth it! Throw in drinking and smoking, as well as being overweight and biting your nails. Despite the commercial with a fetus smoking a cigarette (while drinking a scotch and biting its nails), your parents probably never did any of these things to you, nor did anyone else when you were at an "impressionable" age. Many parents would not teach their kid to smoke anyway.

Current research indicates you are programmed to believe at certain early ages, and programming happens from the outside. You can return to these mental levels via many methods to "re-program" yourself; but what about "bad" habits you picked up later, as opposed to "do as I say and not as I do," or "I'll never wind up doing what they did," but you do so anyway?

When the parents drink and smoke, there is this "do as I say, and NOT as I do" aspect to your programming they installed at an early age. But drinking and smoking are bad habits picked up later, whether or not your parents drank and smoked. By continually doing them, you "later" made the drinking and smoking a habit. You have programmed yourself, and not at the very early age your parents would have done so.

Imagine you had to think about how to drive as if you were going for your driver's test, every time you get in to the car to drive. Check your mirrors, horn, and your seat belt. You might never drive again, but against all odds you do. You have thereby been "programmed" to drive! *Thank doG for parents getting tired of driving kids!*

What about driving a clutch? By the time the belief you can drive a clutch becomes "automatic," you have been programmed by your parents or picked up a new habit, *or maybe someone just needed a new clutch.*

Although I already knew how to drive a clutch, I consciously decided I was tired of shifting when I got my last SUV. BTW, this SUV was markedly lower, especially the headlights in somebody else's rear-view mirror.

Corresponding things "show up" for no reason whatsoever, indicating they come from *Infinity*, which uses no reason or logic. Reflecting "no logic" *Infinity*, I accordingly attracted the occasional "road rager" via my headlights, or so I thought (but some incidents happened during the day).

I don't tailgate nor even follow closely, but I must have believed that driving a truck was attracting the occasional road rager, NOT needing to teach someone a lesson. I even had a saying: "I didn't start it, but I WILL finish it!" after teaching them a lesson, of course, *but the lesson's more for me.*

When you look in a standard mirror, it not only reflects what you have been taught, but also what "comes with the territory" that you couldn't change if you tried (existence in 3D space and time [which is forward-going and linear] are good examples). Some have been said to levitate, but gravity would probably take over if they were pushed out a window 30 stories up … such is my belief. I probably couldn't change these beliefs if I tried.

You have been programmed to believe a lot. The sayings may have originally come from philosophy which does not apply here, since the object is to ultimately change at least some of the outcome. But you probably can't change beliefs that come with the territory.

We have repeatedly been searching for the one right answer, as in I AM *RIGHT*, and everyone and everything else is *WRONG* or just plain stupid. First of all, we need to get rid of the *RIGHT – WRONG* dichotomy which comes along with our culture. This is a belief that seems to come with the territory, but it CAN be changed (if you want).

There may be one RIGHT answer, but it may not be the one you are looking for. Shall we forget about judging a single answer as RIGHT and NOT just a different opinion? To start with, let's list some of what many might consider RIGHT answers. The things our society was born with are RIGHT, are they not? There was something from some religion saying "believing works best" when you act as though you have already received it, so let's look closer. Have we not already received these?

The RIGHT answers would be:
1) The rule of Law (as well as Law itself)
2) Freedom (or individual Liberty)
3) Property Rights (or as it is known today, "Capitalism")

Without one, you can't have any of them. In this *Life* you have people escaping one *Life*, while trying to get to another. People swim, take small boats, or otherwise get close to dying (if they don't actually die) to get to America. Even though they are opposites, "Capitalism" presumably works better than "Communism," but in reality they are just different.

Then there are things that apply to many, but not all. Even so, I doubt you could change a whole culture, even though some individuals have, like Gandhi. In our society, a relatively small group of individuals set up the rule of law, freedom, and property rights for the rest of us. Maybe the belief was popular, judging by people trying anything and everything to get here.

There are more personal things, like the corporation you work for. The smaller the company, the more influence you have. What kind of job do you have? Do you hate your boss or love your boss? What about co-workers? What about going to the job? You will find your beliefs reflect your experience, and vice-versa.

Your choice of a mate, and any kids, obviously involve others. If they are still around, they will be reflected in the mirror of your *Life*. Even if they're not still around, they are in their own *Reality*, and might boomerang back for a do-over. Maybe some buttons just need more pushing, so look in the mirror of *Life*.

There are things that are completely personal, and no-one else is involved – like stopping smoking. You might go into a 7-11 to get a pack or even a carton, but I doubt if the clerk knows your name. This, too, is reflected in the mirror of your *Life*, also whether you are under or over-weight.

Where are you on your *Roadmap-of-Life right now*? Don't know? Well, look in the mirror, which completely and accurately reflects what you are consciously or unconsciously thinking and believing right now, just like the proverbial mirror. How does that work? When you find out, let me know.

This reflection is what you believe about *Reality*, since your beliefs are on automatic and already programmed and mostly unconscious. In fact, you can't consciously think about something and have it happen, or everybody would be rich from playing the lottery *and Government would have shut it down.*

Programming only happens at certain early ages or under certain conditions (according to current research) or else they are habits picked up later. Why would *Life* reflect our thinking so readily? Speculation has one answer: so you can experience ON THE **OUTSIDE** what you are thinking ON THE **INSIDE**.

But said thinking is mostly *unconscious*, whether something has been made visible in our *Reality* from *Infinity* via emotion OR logic. It should be a little easier now to capture the conscious thinking yourself, before it gets thought so many times it becomes an unconscious belief and you have programmed yourself.

How many times have you gone over and over exactly what you are going to say, but somehow it comes out different? Objects materialize when you aren't consciously thinking about them at all! Conscious thinking is left-brain, while unconscious thinking comes from the right. How many times have things shown up you were consciously thinking about?

Things materialize when you are not consciously thinking about them. Maybe nothing "shows up" when you are consciously thinking about it anyway. If you were consciously thinking about it, you would be using words and invoking the logical brain, which is given to be NOT creative.

Of course, shopping for a car involves conscious thinking. But a color, or special deal might "show up" that reflects your unconscious thinking, even if you "thought" you wanted a red Corvette. The right-brain gets involved if you had been meditating on qualities of the ride, or specifics that do not get cancelled out by thoughts like "but I can't afford that!" Facts come along for the ride.

A question often arising in New Thought education: "If our thoughts materialize, how come the occasional thought like 'I wish my boss was dead' doesn't come true?" The answer given was: if all your thoughts came true, you would be living in chaos with pink Elephants showing up in your room at random to talk about. Is that better?

The actual answer is more like: you haven't thought about it long enough so it becomes an automatic, programmed belief showing up with accompanying, corresponding "facts" to reinforce it. Perhaps you have not grown up with the belief "bosses are evil."

Since you can't determine how something will happen, you would feel appropriately guilty if your boss was gunned-down in a botched bank-robbery attempt. But that's only if you thought about it enough to become an automatic belief. And it would probably be something different anyway – like a car crash.

You are now responsible for doing all the things you knew you could do better, now that you are the boss. Bring on the guilt, especially since you were thinking you never considered that part seriously, did you? It would have been better if he just went to another job, especially since he has kids. You might even try to assuage your guilt by buying his kids something.

Some prefer the idea you are living in a movie script of your own *Life* you are writing. It seems to involve less choice, but does it really? Gravity is already reflected in your mirror of *Life*, and you don't have a choice. Who writes in the idea of gravity into a movie script; gravity is assumed to be there regardless. You might watch **Avatar** or the **Harry Potter** films to see if you're afraid of falling if you are totally involved. I don't think anyone wrote gravity into the script.

When you switch between a mirror and a script, always remember the mirror of *Life* is a complete and accurate reflection of your thinking. Any time-delay depends on your belief structure.

A point is worth mentioning. I was busy contemplating an already completed canning of my yard guy for saying he was going to do stuff he never did. I was showering up after completing the 2nd of innumerable back-yard clean-ups my yard guy said he was going to do. First, it was his fault for letting stuff get over-grown, but then I shifted into a mode of personal responsibility; it was ultimately my fault, as I was creating my very-own *Reality*.

I caught myself saying "if I'm doing that" regarding creating *Reality*. Then the old saying went through my mind: "If you want something done (right), you've got to do it yourself." Was *that* still there too? I guess I'll have to work harder on eliminating the old sayings. Was something showing up to confirm that belief and those sayings? *Was it?*

How many other old beliefs, reflected in your sayings, are still in operation? Here's one: they say the "geographic fix" doesn't work, where you move someplace different to guarantee a fix ("unless you believe otherwise" gets quickly added!)

If you leave one place and go another, you will ultimately still be smoking, 50 lbs. overweight, or whatever is reflected in the mirror of your *Life*, unless you "fixed" the problem before you moved. A fix may not be easy, but a geographic fix just doesn't work, or the belief works just the same as it would have otherwise.

A small caveat about the geographic fix. It assumes a "fix" is a rational proceeding, provided by a program you have purchased, wear, or can follow. It will work the same in AK as in FL, or in Europe. This assumes the fix has been provided from the "outside." Buy a spiral-bound map book and change the route-numbers to "conditions to fix." *It might be easier. LOL*

If the fix has been irrationally provided from the inside (without rhyme, reason nor logic), it has come – by definition – from *Infinity* that uses no words nor logic, only emotion. So when the fix has come irrationally, you can go on a cruise around the world as you stop smoking, drinking AND lose weight! You will realize afterward you no longer bite your nails, and are so relaxed! You will also see the world, assuming that, too, came from changing your place on the *Roadmap-of-Life* to a location where you are a healthy, non-smoking world traveler.

There's the old story about FINALLY getting the explanation why everyone cut 4 inches off the roast, when 4 generations of women are in the house at holiday-time. The explanation given to-date was it had always been done that way. Great-grandmother (the eldest) said it would not fit in the only pan they had otherwise!

Do you *believe* you are a good housekeeper? Your house is spotless. If you *believe* you are a good parent, your kids have their hair neatly trimmed when off you go to Grandmother's house on Thanksgiving. I'll bet *your* hair was neatly trimmed when you went to your Grandparent's house for Thanksgiving. Pass the belief on down!

Don't really believe you are a good housekeeper? There's that pile of dirt you have "swept under the rug." We'll leave what parents foist on their kids in terms of the grandkid's hair!

I'm NOT suggesting you let your kid's hair grow wild. Maybe you have the proverbial pile of dirt swept under the rug, but not if you *truly believe* you are a good housekeeper!

It's already true in your *Reality*.

INFINITY AND REALITY TUNE UP

Even though it is often and seemingly interchangeably used, thinking occurs in totally different ways on different sides of the brain (or wherever thinking happens). The word "thinking" usually refers to the step-after-step logical and rational kind of thought, but now you don't have to covet your neighbors stuff. You may think about stealing it via left-brain thinking, but now you can get your own stuff by only changing your location on your *Roadmap-of-Life*. Engaging with even more thinking, the difference between the two types of thinking becomes even more blurred. (Throw the photo out if it's too blurred.)

"Real" items are more than just photographs. That being said, photographs, whether "hard copy," in a scrapbook, or on your iPhone are part of your physical *Reality*. How many times have you looked, even at a scrapbook, sometime after it is done? No matter how many "thumbs up" the pic gets, even the subject of the picture does not look at it for very long. Your relatives will not look at your pics after you're gone, either – that's just *Life*.

Religion once had a monopoly on stories and explanations, but is now challenged by science and other story providers. Science said "OK, we'll take over now and produce measurements, equations, and predictions about how you can make your *Life* happen." But religion and science work on largely different ways of thinking. *Life (The Power of Creation)* and religion continue to evolve.

Consider a couple items currently headlining the "in the NEWS" segment of your *Reality*. It doesn't matter whether they're good or bad, positive or negative, they have some things in common. They are put there by someone else, who decides what stories are deserving of your attention.

It is the belief that attracts visible, personal *Reality* from the invisible, impersonal *Infinity* we all share, via our very own personal *Life*. All beliefs are internal (from the inside) once they have been promoted to a belief and are duly programmed. It is how thoughts get to be a belief that counts. The thoughts can be from the outside, or the inside.

Imagine you have woken up without a single, solitary place to be. You wait a minute to make sure you're not still dreaming. *No place to go?* For most people this would be a Saturday or Sunday. In real *Life*, you can close your eyes while you imagine going back to sleep. *You have closed your eyes again and what you are thinking about is sleep.*

Presumably this is the weekend where you can just lie there and contemplate, and you look around and think "Gee, it would be nice if my religion or any philosophy *AT ALL* could explain how all this stuff got here!" It would be even nicer if that very same philosophy could tell me how to change the things I don't like. Furthermore, you might ask "Is this all there is? Am I still dreaming?"

Instinctively you knew it isn't all there is, you aren't still dreaming, and your *Reality* CAN change (or else you would just be wasting your time reading this). This particular morning you didn't just wake up, turn OFF the alarm clock, and go on autopilot. It would be even worse if you hit the <SNOOZE> button, but it's your *Life* if you choose to snooze through it. On the autopilot mornings, you would be well advised to actually put coffee AND water in the coffee machine, because *it doesn't work well without either.*

But this is the weekend, and you can just lay there thinking. Are there kids? Maybe they'll make coffee. You actually think you can smell coffee brewing, or maybe you're still on the verge of dreaming. As the fog lifts from your brain, you try to remember if you have one of those coffee machines with a clock you can set to make coffee automatically; you can remember looking at one.

Smelling coffee brewing is only the faintest of hopes if you don't have a coffee machine with a clock, nor can you remember if there are any kids awake and capable of operating Mr. Coffee. The fog lifts further as you try to remember if there are any kids; maybe they are off to college *and have their own barista.*

But today you don't go back to sleep, and instead revisit some of the things you saw in the brief moment you had your eyes open. Next to your bed, there is a table with a bunch of half-read books and their bookmarks, a light by which you can read them, and someone is still sleeping on the other side of the bed. Maybe there isn't anyone there.

Perhaps you like the still-sleeping person, but there are those times you think you could do better. Maybe there was no-one over there and you wished there were. You can imagine what they would be like after you have changed them (as well as yourself, but that's harder). It's easy changing them, or at least providing suggestions. *The old joke goes: a woman marries a man hoping he'll change, but he doesn't; and a man marries a woman hoping she'll never change, but she does!*

Wouldn't it be nice, you contemplate, if there were a philosophy that told you how stuff got here (or didn't, as in the case of a missing sleeper?) Nothing you encountered to date seems to fit the bill in that regard. Even better would be a philosophy that would tell you how you could change to *other* stuff if you didn't like your current situation. You sigh contentedly as you fluff up your pillow with your arm and drift off back to sleep.

Potentially, you don't completely like the person still asleep next to you, and wish they were someone else, unless, of course, they made coffee just this once. If they did, we'll give them a pass. Perhaps there is no one there and you wish there were. *A coffee machine with a clock and timer would be cheaper than a real person, logic tells you.*

We noted *Infinity* is invisible, *Reality* is visible, and *Life* referees between invisible and visible. Although *Infinite*, you have a single *Reality* governing your *Life* (we ditched multiple *Realities* as unknowable), but the bumper sticker still says: "Life's a Beach and Then You Die!" Someone put bumper stickers into our visible *Reality*.

We have but three pieces of existence: *Infinity*, *Reality*, and *Life*. There ... just said it succinctly without thousands upon thousands of pages and explanations. Although *Reality*, and *Life*, come from *Infinity* and can accommodate all explanations and possibilities, they remain simple, yet ironically, infinite.

Being incarnate at the moment, I must have come here to be the never married son who has doGs instead of kids. This would be connected somehow to one of my lessons. Maybe I'll get married and adopt. For the next *Life*, I'll be the daughter; it seems easier. But with all the hardships accommodating women, I may have to re-think that. It will be a hoot figuring it all out between lives anyway. *Once you're dead, you're dead, but* (as Arnold in **The Terminator** says) *"I'll be back"!*

A philosophy must exist where there has to be at least one "ah, shit" nanosecond accompanying death. It doesn't matter if you were standing at ground zero in a nuclear explosion, or were riding the bomb down, slapping the side with your Cowboy Hat (**Dr. Strangelove**). You're still dead, so can't you have that "ah shit" nanosecond too? Even if you're stoned to death (*and I don't mean getting so stoned you die!*) once you're dead, you're dead, but you can come back!

We have all come from *Infinity*, regardless of whether we are now visible or not, predicated on whether our consciousness entity wants to also be visible in our *Reality* and "learn its lessons." Remember: there are those that want to fight over the "G" word. That might be *their* lesson.

Since we started with *Infinity*, it would be appropriate to add the visible "state" of *Reality* into the mix somewhere: here is as good a place as any! Although *Life* is more of a process than a state, *Life* still needs to go somewhere too.

"State" seems to imply a static existence, even if it includes everything, as *Infinity* does. Since first conceptualizing a "state," the realization came that the word itself had come from the description of the **zero state** described in ***Zero Limits*** [6]. The ho'oponono philosophy refers to a state where all existence is, right before the "Big Bang," or however one wants to refer to the intrusion of *Reality* and *Life*.

But nothing is static, and depends on your state of consciousness to determine your basic existence. So the word "existence" gets substituted for "state," and instead of states, everyone has three "pieces of existence" (*Infinity, Reality, Life*) where static is NOT a factor; such are the three infinite "*Pieces of Existence*" we get, whether we want them or not, when we are "here" to express *Reality* and *Life* for 100 Years (or less).

---

[6] Vitale, Joe; Len, Ihaleakala Hew. Zero Limits: The Secret Hawaiian System for Wealth, Health, Peace, and More (pp. 169-170). Wiley. Kindle Edition.

When we are invisible and not in form, we have only *Infinity* which has no time, only eternity. Of course, we could always consider eternity as a really, really long time. Clock time is an aspect of our *Reality* that normally operates via words and logic. *A commercial comes to mind where one of the side effects of a sleep-aid: causes occasional death. That's a really long dirt-nap.*

Even when we are in the world of words, logic, and reason, *Infinity* has no words or euphemisms to explain it; in fact, *Infinity* has no words nor logic *at all*, only emotions. *Infinity* can be alluded to via words, but try to use words to explain "puppy love." That would be when you are "in love" listening non-stop to the AM love-song radio station ... *but who could understand* that *anyway?*

Being "in love" comes close to the ultimate *Love* factor used by *Life*, but try to explain either with words. Words usually come complete with logic and reason, but are largely *Infinities* opposite as words are replaced with emotional "thinking." Try using words to explain:
- The smell of a Rose (by any other name it still smells as sweet)
- The taste of asparagus (even if it causes your pee to smell!)
- The feel of fear.

You cannot use words to communicate emotions or *Infinity*. You can allude to *Infinity*, but there are no words to communicate: sights, sounds, smell, taste, and feelings. *Can you name the missing physical sense?*

Sight, sound, smell, taste, with touch bringing in what is physically missing. These are the physical senses granted us upon our birth arrival in form from *Infinity* that allow us to move around. We also consider what is delivered to us via our senses to be identical as what the senses brings everyone else. So what two or more people see, must be the same, right?

Same with hear, smell and the rest of the senses. But senses are *not* identical! They pass through interpretation by our brain. The very same hill will look steeper to the very same person that has just finished working out. Rock music will sound like a bunch of broken strings to one, where opera sounds melodious to him. One person loves rock-and-roll and hates opera, while the other loves opera and can't stand rock-and-roll. If all senses had no interpretation, they would be the same facts. That must be why the police ask for two or more descriptions of the same accident.

Studies have shown that some senses, hearing in particular, are in operation from conception on. The creation in the womb knows the difference between an argument between the parents fighting and classical music, so they say. Supposedly events can be "proven" that the womb-ster hears, and there are undoubtedly some making other things up. So we will start with an event that cannot be categorically denied – the birth of the infant. It's one of those unchangeable facts where everyone has a birthday *(even if you're female, and the birth-year keeps changing to keep you 39!)*

We learn how to use our senses over the first couple years to navigate *Reality*, even if senses get interpreted, and rules get subsequently added like "look both ways before crossing." Those are just rules, no-one teaches us how to look, and our beliefs teach us how to interpret sensual input.

Emotions are closest to a non-physical sense (which is one reason why we use *sense*), allowing communication back-and-forth from the non-physical *Infinity* to our physical *Reality* by *Life*, but emotions are largely unexplored in our culture. One major exception: the emotions of anger and joy are "permitted" with sporting events. Apparently people (usually men) get REALLY-PISSED-OFF (the emotion of self-righteous anger) when your team loses, especially when it's YOUR TEAM ! ! !

If there is the tiniest chance that something happens, theory has it that it happens for sure in *Infinity*. And not only does it happen just once, but it happens an infinite number of times. *Tell me that doesn't bend your logical brain!*

Infinity is endless; there are no limits to what is contained in *Infinity*. If you have any idea about what might be *different* about *Infinity*, you would need to express your ideas and research the concept again, but you will probably come around to the preceding view. But *Infinity* is big enough to handle disparate views. *Infinity* is infinite, and the infinite contains all possibilities, so it can handle different views too.

To continue with *Infinity*, since it is infinite, you cannot sub-divide it. There is not half over here, and half over there, and in the same manner, you can't multiply it. There are not two, nor any other number of infinities – just one. If there were multiple infinities, there might be part over here, and part over there, but there isn't. The same would seem to hold true regarding *Infinity* within a *Reality*, but the jury is still out regarding multiple *Realities*. Still remember: not long ago we were all "flat earthers!"

Infinity itself is an amorphous blob that is invisible, not in form, is everywhere and nowhere, and all that. It has no words, explanations, time-frames, or anything else logical. It is like the heretofore little mentioned "G" word. *Hint: it's your doG, complete with unconditional Love. Woof!*

This amorphous blob has nothing else <u>but</u> *Infinite* stuff. No words, no reason, no time, nada. That being said, we can look at *Infinity* as having coarse, as well as more refined properties. The coarse continuum meets the basic requirements of being invisible and everywhere, and gets refined into more and more discrete and specific personal elements. They may also cross into elements of another property – that's OK by the rules too. Sometimes a possibility may become a probability and even visible in *Reality*.

To start off, *Infinity* has limitless possibilities and endless ideas, where endless ideas are possibilities first cousin. No matter what you multiply (expand) or divide (contract) something in *Infinity* by, you still get *Infinity*. Of course, there are sub-divisions within each possibility or idea. How else could you get anything discrete out of just a possibility?

The words side of our brain wants to differentiate *Infinity* so we can talk about it. We need to be careful when we switch between *Infinity* and *Reality*, which can happen quite easily. The easiest way to tell which one we are thinking about is whether or not it is visible.

If what we are "thinking" about is invisible and everywhere, we are thinking about *Infinity*. If something is visible, we are thinking about *Reality*. There are more characteristics, but visibility is the easiest one to latch onto. Besides the basic requirements of *Infinity* (invisible, formless, everywhere), what might its other properties be? *This is a question for you to answer.*

Speaking of *Infinity*, a little "understanding" might be in order. Understanding is in quotes, because it comes from the logical, rational side of our brain, as do the words we use. Continuum may be a word we can use to allude to *Infinity* or the things contained within. Discrete is a word better suited to *Reality*.

One property of the invisible *Infinite* is energy, which can be subdivided (or refined) into electrical energy, or *doG forbid* "fossil fuel." The planet has been orbiting the Sun for 4.5 Billion years doing something. Said electrical energy can then be stored in batteries to be used by your remote control, laptop or Tesla cars. Since the battery itself, as well as the remote control, laptop, and Tesla cars themselves belong in *Reality*, they are visible. Nicola Tesla himself has re-entered the invisible *Infinite*, after leaving us with some of his ideas – alternating current (AC) is one of them. (*No, the car is just named after him, he didn't have that idea!*)

This property of electrical energy is combined with the concept of storing said energy, which crosses a property boundary or line, and remains quite legal. The two get merged together to give us our battery. We can then operate our clicker (or is that an "old" word?) *Even though the remote may seem invisible at times, it is really just hiding somewhere in the couch cushions.*

Another example might help illustrate the difference between *Infinity* and *Reality*. The idea of flight is an idea contained within *Infinity*. Once it is moved into the visible by the Wright brothers, flight is now firmly ensconced in *Reality*. The idea has now been layered upon other ideas, which have been firmly entrenched in their visible counterparts after they have been created from ideas in *Infinity*.

Of course, what is contained within any individual property of the *Infinite* is infinite, and can only be alluded to by words. Since the *Infinite* cannot be totally comprehended by the finite, we'll just say there are LOTS of course properties and even finer sub-divisions within any given property. The finite brain can wrap its arms around LOTS, which is why we use that word to allude to infinite quantities.

The formless and in-form ideas move back and forth between *Infinity* and *Reality*, and become products in our *Reality*. This is how many people seem to come up with the "same idea" almost simultaneously. They are all tapped into shared *Infinity* from their personal *Realities*.

One of the requirements for membership in the *Infinite* is no matter what you multiply or divide it by (expand or contract it) you still get the same thing. Silence is a good example. Expand or contract silence, and you still get silence.

To paraphrase the line in the commercial "Can you hear me now?" in the negative, "I still can't hear you, and all there is *is* silence." Perhaps you need more bars, which are either the kind on your phone or the kind with alcohol. *People talk a lot in the alcohol kind of bar, but unfortunately a lot of the talk seems to fall into the same sort of talk as what size fish got away.*

One of the LOTS of properties the amorphous *Infinite* blob has is consciousness. Consciousness is invisible and everywhere, but a consciousness entity is more refined and personal, and even becomes visible when born. "Consciousness entity" differentiates between entities, and this includes pets and everything else with consciousness – LOTS and LOTS of consciousness entities.

For the sake of this discussion and relative simplicity, as well as retain the "center of everything" hubris, we will limit ourselves to the human "brand" of consciousness entity. As such, there are LOTS of them visible right now – enough to keep us busy – 6, 7, or 8 billion of them on the planet *right now*!

Just remember the easy rule – if it's invisible (formless) and everywhere at once (no place it isn't), chances are good it belongs in *Infinity*! We just need to assign duality words to allude to it so we can talk about it using reason and logic, and thus move it into *Reality*. Next we'll discuss the third state of existence – *Life*.

MORE ON LIFE

When you "pop out" of the womb, you are an open book ready to be programmed. Right now we are concerned with original programming. Current studies show the frequency of the brain, and at what age you are most likely, and what your normal hindrances are to programming, *as well as how to get back to a certain frequency to re-program yourself.*

Habits are picked up later. Can you tell me anything in your *Life* (excluding original programming) that did not get there as a direct result of your actions? How did *that* happen? Did somebody else put something there for you to, say, trip over? You are tripping over your *Life* right now.

Your *Life* is spent perceiving (looking at, thinking about) your mental creations, which you might assume are more than just perceptions as you are physical.

> *Time it was, and what a time it was ... I have a photograph*
> *Preserve your memories ... that's all that's left you*
> **Simon and Garfunkel; *Bookends***

But when you're physical no longer, even your pics don't go with you. Remember the old saying: "You can't take it with you?" It does not apply just to money and things bought via the money model. Read on if you want to change your *Life* while you're still in it.

84

Take your Job, Career, and Salary as one example where *Life* has been misconstrued. *Life*, here, indicates it is the third "piece of existence," and is more like a process than something static. To continue with the example tailored to logical thinking, consider your salary.

You have a job with a salary which can make the invisible visible, let's say via a new car you can purchase. With it might come a McMansion with a three-car garage and a spot on Oprah, to say nothing of a new wife.

Anything having to do with anything is about *Life*, hence the thousands upon thousands of pages and explanations religions have associated with them making it easier to go from the invisible, to the measured and predictable visible world. People like making things visible (as <whatever> goes from *Infinity* to *Reality* via the celestial librarian called *Life*) and the word meta-physics gets accordingly assigned.

A belief is a thought that has been thought so many times you need to consciously think it no longer. The belief makes *Life* simpler by being internal, and by the time a thought becomes a belief, you have been programmed. And that programming comes complete with filters and *Life* provides reinforcement. Let's back up a step and consider the original thought.

How does the original thought happen? Hint: by your perception. How does perception happen? Hint: via your senses. How do your senses get there? Hint: you are born with them. So you are a consciousness entity born with perception.

Imagine you were born one minute ago. *Life*, in form, is so amazing! How do you differentiate between a human that is able to take care of your needs from all the other shapes and colors present? From your senses – sight at first. Crying helps, and we have added sound. All the other senses are eventually added, if they aren't already there.

Your needs are met, and you can layer one belief on top of another, like this is a good human, and this is a bad human. Good and bad are emotional beliefs layered on top of all the other senses. Perception IS *Reality*, by now it is complete and programmed, and able to be layered. There is more than just sensual perception.

While you're alive, you can communicate with "the great beyond" via your emotions, says the Law of Attraction (LOA). LOA also says limit your emotions to "good" and "bad," [7] otherwise there are just too many possibilities. ***The Course in Miracles*** says we only bring "Love" (a "good" creation) with us; maybe a bad emotion is just our "soul" saying "No! I don't want that!" Given our physical senses, plus our emotional ability to communicate with *Infinity*, why does our seemingly single and simple *Life* seem so incomplete and painful? Maybe because we don't use what we were given. *We are, after all, only human.*

Take the current model for advertisements, appealing to independent observers having their beliefs and *Life* coming at them from the outside. Just do as they say, which could be called the parental approach (all you need to remember is NOT do what your parents actually do). Simple.

When the blue pill first appeared, you were supposed to go the ER if you had more than a four-hour "erection." My first thought would have been to go to the Guinness Book of World Records. *A comedian said he would call three other women after an hour with the first one.*

---

[7] Esther Hicks;Jerry Hicks. Ask and It Is Given: Learning to Manifest Your Desires (all Kindle Locations). Kindle Edition.

Now they have a pill you can take a day ahead of time, and they have largely eliminated the ER suggestion, but if you can walk around for a day with an erection, who knows? First there was Junior High; maybe now you're proud to "get it up," which is a good thing, isn't it? You don't even need a notebook to cover it up any longer. Wouldn't you be proud to change your *Life* for the better?

They are now selling something that can give you an erection in your sleep. I think I'll spend more time sleeping! But wait, doesn't that already happen when you're dreaming? Aren't you proud to be an American!

Remember: **You CAN Get There** from here!

REALITIES

We live in a *Reality* that has forward-going linear time. It is impossible to realize anything different. Do you get the phonetic link between *Reality* and realize? If you had taken Latin that made you aware of base words, you might recognize "real" as the base. *Really.*

There is proof of alternate *Realities.* A long time ago, **Time** magazine called them different dimensions. Pilots have observed UFOs making right-angle turns at high speeds, far outside our laws of physics. Note the plural of pilot, so you would NOT consider these observations as one-off occurrences.

If you think these pilots are whack-jobs where something about flying makes you wacky, you might never want to fly again. Otherwise, consider these observances as objects slightly entering our *Reality*, while still observing their own rules. This is what **Time** related as an "explanation." *Area 51 comes to mind. There is also an "area 52" for all the left-over stuff.*

Different channeled sources also report multiple *Realities.* Seth mentions one in an almost offhand way. **The Seth Material** reports some *Realities* operate in a forward-going linear time-frame, but there are other *Realities* in which time goes *backwards*, so Seth says.

There is another "character" known in **The Seth Material** as *Seth II* who comes infrequently through Seth. He is supposed to come from a *Reality* as far on the other side of Seth as Jane is to Seth. We are told not to even try to understand his *Reality* via our usual methods, so *Seth II* is therefore largely unknown and unknowable. *That's all I know. LOL*

Such is another *Reality*, not to be "understood" from our own *Reality*, with the exception of understanding linear time (one event occurs after another). In our *Reality* time goes forward, and in other *Realities* time goes backward, therefore linear time would dictate events occur one *before* the other there. What's to understand, anyhow?

If you wonder what might be different about time going backwards, consider birth and death. Death comes first, and life ends in an orgasm. *Comedians have already come up with that!* You might start to understand, but understanding may only be part of our *Reality*. Who knows what other differences from our *Reality* there might be, or if we could "understand" any of them. Understanding using words and reason may only be an aspect of our *Reality*.

We might be most correct, however, calling Reality *Realities* and Life would be *Lives* in the plural version, and be best at capturing *Infinity*, but we'll stick with the singular for ease and clarity of the following discussion.

In the Law of Attraction materials, the not-in-form entities of Abraham are asked what the base laws of our Universe are. They (Abraham) expect people are looking for answers like: 3D space; time (add the forward-going and linear part); gravity; etc. but Abraham is quick to state these are only *agreements* used to communicate these laws.

Abraham states the *same three* fundamental laws exist in EVERY *Reality* (which are NOT the same as the *agreements* we all hold dear in our *Reality*). The fundamental laws are:

1) The Law of Attraction
2) The Science of Deliberate Creation, and
3. The Art of Allowing [8]

Review the Law of Attraction (Abraham) materials (noted in **Suggestions** …) for more information.

We previously made a point via the multi-dimensional Roadmap. The analogy has routes running together, splitting apart, and possibly running back together again (for a do-over) in people's lives. In actuality, many of our own situations resemble this occurrence, thus the analogy holds true.

So if you have a bad relationship, it may end, then run back together for a do-over. If there are kids involved, they get their own route numbers which fade into the background; maybe onto another page. Of course, there are no route numbers on an actual *Roadmap-of-Life*; the signs would be conditions-of-existence instead, but we will keep the numbers in this analogy.

It doesn't matter if the parents have a do-over or not in their existence, that's not the point. Nor, in *Reality* are the kids getting another chance to push the parents' buttons, or vice-versa. The important point is everyone's map intersects everyone else's at different points on this roadmap. *Most likely everyone is pushing everyone else's buttons anyhow.*

The Law of Attraction tells us we also have LOTS of existences. We start from an invisible *Infinity*, then add the parts that correspond to our visible *Reality*, via *Life*. To keep things as simple as possible, we will assume a single *Life* and *Reality* for the time being; the fly in the ointment are all those other pesky *Realities* (not considered here).

---

[8] Hicks, Esther; Jerry Hicks. The Law of Attraction (all pages). Hay House, Inc. - A. Kindle Edition.

Having nothing else to go on, we can assume other *Realities* have something similar to the process we call *Life* that brings their *Reality* forth and makes it visible, but maybe not. Some *Realities* may exist totally in the *Infinite* and the frustrating point is our *inquiring minds will never know.*

Proving something may be in our *Reality*, maybe it *only* gets proven here, and possibly the only part that will ever be "proved" is in our *Reality* anyway! Come up with an equation for anything and everything going on, even in our *Reality*. GO AHEAD! One really requires an open mind to even begin to grasp *Infinity*.

Close your eyes for a moment and <u>imagine</u> (*imagination* is part of the *Infinite*, as per its invisibility, etc.) the *Life* you would like to lead. It doesn't matter what is (or isn't) in your *Life* right now. You are writing a brand-new script for a movie, and the movie is your *Life*. You might consider the script as totally make-believe, but it can be so much more, and will be if you want.

The movie script, which includes optional and changeable parts, will become a mirror that reflects back your thinking, which is often below the level of your consciousness. These beliefs become automatic once they are duly programmed and internal. As Wayne Dyer says, "Our Beliefs about Ourselves are the Most Telling Factors in Determining our Level of Success & Happiness in Life" [9]

Try to imagine there are LOTS of consciousness entities *within* your very own single *Reality*. That might be a stretch, but you can do it. Use the 100-Year rule: at the beginning of the 100 years gone by, you weren't here either, were you?

"Here" refers to being in physical existence. You weren't here 100 years ago, and you won't be here in another 100 years, such is my

[9] Wayne Dyer quotes (Kindle Location 828). Kindle Edition.

100-Year Rule. Think of all your relatives that have come before or will presumably come after. Where did everybody go? Back to where they came from.

According to Einstein, energy cannot be created nor destroyed, it can only change form. Therefore, there is a *"Life* energy" present in every visible consciousness entity. Actual *Life* occurs when a consciousness entity decides to be born, and at the very least have *Life's* lessons presented. The accompanying physical senses are born as well, including the non-physical "sense" of emotion. At the same time *Life* reflects back our one-and-only visible *Reality*.

In the same *Reality*, the base laws of existence people ask Abraham to provide, are nothing more than *agreements*. These are things like: 3D space and gravity; other laws-of-physics we use would be agreements also. It should be clear these *agreements* are different from the three laws present in all *Realities*; these basic three laws are in our *Reality* also – *they can't NOT be.*

You might live in the same place before you decide to change locations, or you might decide to move someplace different. If your health is currently good, then it probably remains unchanged. Why would anyone want to downgrade their good health, which might be impossible anyway, since perfect health is an aspect of creation. If your health is currently bad, it might be one of those things you want to change for the better, especially if you are going to physically move. If you have kids, you'll probably still have them too, *unless you decide to move somewhere they can never find you!*

The rest of *Reality* (including the non-agreements laws) always remain more-or-less the same. "More-or-less" excludes the details. If you wish to change from forward-going linear time, or any of the other agreements we have, you'll have to change *Realities*, and not just move within the one already occupied. That is not the objective of this reading, and we wouldn't even know what another *Reality* would look like. There are plenty of changes we can make within our single *Reality*, which is our goal.

Let's have a lesson. In Seth, he said we move into physical *Reality* to "learn lessons," whatever they might be. Let's try one fictional lesson on for size. In our *Reality*, there is one-and-only-one position to be filled, we'll call it President of the US. There are two competing parties, each with two candidates, one of which will reach the final election stage. The parties are mutually exclusive, as are the four candidates themselves. Only one party, with one candidate, can ultimately hold the position. So our lesson has four mutually exclusive possibilities.

> *Sitting on a sofa on a Sunday Afternoon. Going to the candidates' debate.*
> *Laugh about it ... shout about it ... when you've got to choose. Any way you look at it you lose!*
> ### *Simon and Garfunkel;* **Mrs. Robinson**

You have a friend that holds a diametrically opposed view, does this exercise, then an election happens. It is equally important to each that their ideology, political policies, and candidate "wins." They each move into a *Reality* that includes the election of "their" candidate. Don't forget each makes his own *Reality* from scratch.

Does that mean in each of the cases, the losing friend will "disappear" from the other's view predicated on the prevailing party ideology? Not necessarily. Let's assume that in either of the two cases the "supporter's" candidate gets elected, the economy is robust, so one person can justifiably prove to the other they are *RIGHT* and the other is *WRONG*!

This also assumes importance to both proving they are *RIGHT*, and the other is *WRONG*. Remember, in each of the four *Realities* corresponding to the four possibilities things go merrily along. *McLaughlin would be proud of all the RIGHTness and WRONGness!*

Chances are good somewhere along the line things are not equal, as they never are in *Infinity*. So while one friend may not "disappear," they will fade in importance as one candidate gets elected, and the economy gets better or worse. Each person is now in one of eight (or more) options corresponding to the candidate, the economy, etc. Another option depends on how important it is for one friend to prove to the other how *WRONG* they are, and how the wrong friend takes it. He might just disappear! Who wants to be continually reminded they are WRONG?

Add other options to just two friends, two parties, four candidates, their policies and the economy, and you can see where possibilities and *Realities* quickly become *Infinite*.

So *Reality* and *Life* is different for each person, and ultimately goes back into the *Infinite* we all share!

You CAN Get There from here!

JUDGE NOT, LEST YE BE JUDGED

A Christmas gift book for unexpected visitors was acquired at a local bookstore; it is called *Gifts from a Course in Miracles*. Every page had a subject and quotation from the Course, and on the facing page is a drawing or photograph (in Black &White) to reinforce the quote, or provide a focus for meditation.

Upon arriving home, a decision was made to peruse the book. On the first page opened to, the subject was **Judgment** with the accompanying quote and picture. Opening to a second entry, a second page was examined … the subject was **Judgment**, except with a different quote and picture, but still no cause for alarm. Another page was flipped to … the subject was **Judgment** with yet another quote and picture. Wait a flying minute, was this whole book about *Judgment*? But it wasn't, according to the table of contents. That particular episode was not easily forgotten (and the book, with its "lessons" is still on my shelf). Why did the book keep opening to judgment?

There are judgmental people. The very first thing they notice about someone is whether they are short/tall, fat/skinny, black/white, etc. I am not even embarrassed to tell a fat joke to people whom others would judge "fat," even if the joke later causes some awkwardness.

Apparently part of the human condition is a need to feel superior to others, or at least be *RIGHT*. Whatever the superiority concept might be (health, wealth, power, et al), one can easily find somebody else who is indeed superior, as well as boat-loads of people that are inferior. If you feel having wealth makes you superior, you will easily find someone that has more. If you feel having a great body makes you superior, look no further than Arnold (he's not near #1 anymore!) Politics is useful whereby your side has all the great ideas, and the other side is wrong.

There it is: the other side is just plain stupid. That may be *my* particular superiority concept: mental IQ power as determined by somebody. After all, I was in the "smartest" section of school from the 7th grade until graduation from High School, even after some later events should have excluded me from that section. Just show me one instance – only one – where your philosophy has worked. Otherwise YOU are just plain stupid. See how superiority works?

Wallowing in *RIGHTness* is something that can be done all day. Maybe that is what the book was saying: one can be judgmental without even knowing it. The book is still on my shelves, and I have never forgotten the "lesson."

While writing this, a trash-truck came through our local community. Others might earlier have judged the driver as a "poor schlub" driving a trash truck (but at least he was not on the back!) Now, he is one-of-the-select few who was chosen to drive a truck and push a button. Now the "poor schlubs" are hanging off the back of a competitor's truck coming through later, according to the "poor schlub" judgment.

Infinity contains all these types of consciousness: wealth, health, brain-power, etc. A friend had a car upon which was plastered the name of the dealer: "Judge." It always reminded to "Judge not, or else you will be judged [SIC]." Give up on judgment is what that book may have been indicating a long, long time ago. My smell checker flags neither the "ye" nor the "lest" part, therefore they must be "legal" in the following statement: "Judge not, lest ye be judged" (you know it is scripture because of the "ye" and "lest" parts, and comes complete with a first-person affirmation).

Has being smarter or dumber than anyone else actually helped or hindered *anyone*? Some people have more-or-less all the judgment concepts rolled-up in one compact place. If you can't find anything else about the other to judge them by, perhaps they have more compassion. Wait a flyin' minute: is compassion a judgement topic?

A further thought is presented. "Do what you love and you'll never work another day." Did someone say that? The word "work" is in there, which has judgment rolled into the word. One of the most popular current authors presumably doing what she loves is JK Rowling, and her Harry Potter series. JK Rowling could also be judged as superior to most in the wealth department.

Do you suppose she judged [10] any of the characters as superior or inferior to any of the others while she was writing these works, despite whether some might be judged an eventual "winner" (Harry Potter) or "loser" (his step-parents)? No language implying judgment can be easily found. Maybe it's not winners or losers that matter, it's just that the characters are different!

So turn off any judgment while you are writing your movie script, especially about yourself. Do you think any movie-script-writers would be successful while being judgmental about the different characters in the script? How many times does the "bad" guy turn out to be the "good" guy? Maybe the characters are simply different!

---

[10] Hicks, Esther; Jerry Hicks. The Law of Attraction (all pages). Hay House, Inc. - A. Kindle Edition.

How many people would go see a movie where the characters were all the same? There was that MTV video long ago where all the dancing babes were supposed to be the same, as well as the occasional NEWS blurb where they have all the North Korean soldiers goose-stepping as they bounce in tandem with their heads cocked 45-degrees to the right, doing the Heil-Hitler salute. Is that supposed to be impressive or scary? Maybe the characters are just different! In 100 Years no-one will care.

It's time to stop being judgmental, especially about yourself in your own Step Two script. Now for some irony. Let's *judge* others as WRONG or just plain stupid in real life, shall we?

Upon listening to a 1995 interview on YouTube! with George Soros (with that much money he can't be just plain stupid, can he?) Charlie Rose found out *both* Capitalism and Communism were WRONG according to Soros, so let's have the context. You can find this interview on youTube! if you look hard enough.

George said (toward the beginning of the interview) charity was bad for both the giver AND receiver. The receiver forgot how to look out for themselves, and just slopped up to the trough. The receiver proceeded to tell the giver everything he wanted to hear.

A little economics was thrown in of the limited pie variety, ultimately replaced by growing the size of the pie whereby everybody gets a bigger piece. George *said* he was skilled at assessing change, and the Internet was poised to replace printing as a man-made change agent producing a bigger pie. Was he all that different in 1995?

The reason for watching: currently Soros is judged by conservatives as the epitome of evil, funding all sorts of subversive communist-type activities with his immense wealth. (He did explain what he was doing with his well-known attempt at cornering of the British

Sterling market.) He was 65 in 1995, which makes him 85+ now, and is still doing the same thing. (His *Reality* is created by him.) First we'll *judge* him as WRONG, then back off and say he is just different.

There was a huge Maple Tree next door. It would take more than two people to encircle the trunk with their arms, near the bottom of the tree. The branches going out above the height of my head were limbs as big as a normal tree trunk. Unfortunately, a storm took it out – such is the nature of permanency.

Squirrels would run round-and-round playing (or maybe they were courting, as squirrels do in their inimitable way) and were visible from my bed many mornings. In the fall, the tree would release thousands upon thousands (maybe millions) of twirly-birds to come to rest wherever they may; many would come to rest in my garden and take root. The tree didn't care.

Let's say besides being a mother-maple tree, it is also a tree of economics and politics. There is an entire branch full of twirly-birds for private property and what is currently known as capitalism; the same goes for communism. Other branches hold all the accumulated knowledge represented by different forms of Utopia. Some will make it, some won't.

Someone needs to point out which one of the twirly-birds will make it, and which ones won't. There would be a line where those on this side survive, those landing on the other side of the line will perish. This would also imply a judgment: this way is *RIGHT* and the other way is *WRONG*!

Of course people want to be on the *RIGHT* side, but the Universe doesn't care! Only the strongest and best survive, regardless of all else. Such is the nature of evolution as it continues to move forward in our *Reality*.

Religious Science principles state that every fraction-of-an-ounce twirly-bird has the potential, given the right conditions, of becoming a multi-ton behemoth mother tree, releasing its own twirly-birds. There is no way to know whether that ever happened from this particular tree, but one thing *can* be known: every tree that took root was different. None were *RIGHT* and none were *WRONG*. They were just different.

The question of doubting any results you achieve upon doing this exercise will come up, adding reinforcement. Just keep watching the results, and doubts will disappear. What we are talking about are a couple easy steps, minus the mental discipline needed to carry them out. Doing so is easy, once you have gotten in tune with *Infinity* and *Reality*.

You CAN Get There from here!

SOUNDS GOOD!

The Sun is a mega power-generating-machine. We will say the sun gives off Ziga-Watts of power (we are using a "Z" since it is the last letter in the alphabet). It cannot be truly infinite since it is visible and in our *Reality*, even though they tell you not to look at it. It might as well be invisible except during an eclipse (then they tell you not to look at it too). It just sits there doing its thing night and day, 24 / 7. Just remember not to look directly at it!

There we sit, visible if at all, from the sun's vantage point. You will have your face warmed in the daytime by the sun, when you face it. Since the earth spins on its axis, the side facing the sun is in daytime, the other side night; but for the sun, there is only daytime.

By the time it gets here, the power given off by the sun to its barely visible neighbor will have been stepped down from ziga-watts to (let's say) giga-watts, still enough to power everything from some solar-cells in the NV desert, so they tell us. There was even some investor who was ready to go for powering everything by sun-generated electricity, but he could not get the rights-of-way for the power lines. Maybe his mistake was not to claim "free," which is always a popular selling point. If you bother to look at TV advertising, you will note many advertised items have something "free" attached. BTW, did someone not say "There ain't no free lunch?"

They told us we would have 1000 by (the year) 2000 and "free" power. 1000 referred to nuclear reactors, but instead we got Chernobyl and Three-Mile Island. I think the 1000 Freebie promise was made by Nixon, whom everybody loves to hate, but he's in form no longer anyway, which doesn't stop anybody from hating him. Apparently "they" are politicians making promises they can't keep, but where would we be without them?

Then there's the wind farm that no-one wants in their backyard. Killing off a few endangered species of birds is OK if you are going for the greater good of renewable energy, just don't shoot anything. Teddy Roosevelt said it is OK to shoot anything, anytime. "Bully" Teddy said. *Perhaps bullying and the 2nd Amendment started their bad rap at the same time.*

Regarding "renewable energy" from solar cells or wind farms, there's only one thing they forgot to tell us: "What do you do on a cloudy, windless day?" Our planet has been sitting here for a couple billion years as a battery charged by the sun, even though it's not the kind of battery that goes in remote controls, laptops or Tesla cars. Our planet is the kind of battery that stores energy in Plankton that go to the bottom and eventually turns into Coal or Oil to get recovered and burned as "fossil fuels," which someone figured out were high in stored energy.

Yecch. Even if it is smelly, the energy works the same on a rainy day as a sunny one, with or without wind. BTW, the first cars were electric and we are going back to that now, even if electric cars are ultimately powered by fossil fuels. Yecch.

There were no words or standard left-brain logic involved when the planet was sitting around charging up in an illogical sort-of way. Nobody cared if it was cloudy and rainy, even for several days, or even weeks, in a row. Words were in the distant future.

In fact, it was long before dinosaurs when this was originally occurring, and still is and will be. No words or logic could be involved, and it is easy to say there was only *Infinity* then. Then someone comes along having two sides to their brain, and attempts to solve the rainy-day problem. Just store-up enough energy to carry us through cloudy windless days, and we are now firmly in the logical world of words trying different technologies for batteries.

Storing energy works directly with the logical side of life, and you will probably notice that using renewable energy and electric cars makes you feel good. Feeling good would be your connection to the *Infinite* via emotions, according to the Law of Attraction (LOA). But there's still one thing missing according to the LOA: the third Law. Law #3 is The Art of Allowing, even when it appears "they" are trying to disallow your freedom of choice.

Suspicions have it politicians will try to force everyone into using the same source-of-power … it's their model. But people want to use whatever works best among several options for them, under the circumstances. It is no business of anyone's that someone is trying to buy a pack of Camel non-filter electric vapes, any more than it would be if the table was turned and someone is buying an actual pack of Camel non-filters. But politicians don't want anyone doing anything without their permission (you might brand them "control freaks.")

It might be easier to change to a different spot on the *Infinite Roadmap-of-Life*, where you are using as much renewable energy as possible, with remaining electricity from fossil fuels. Figure out the details and whether you feel good about doing it later, if you "feel" like it!

But … ***You CAN Get There*** from here!

THE SAME AS EVERYBODY ELSE

We know everyone is different. We also know there is supposed to be safety in numbers. At the very least this safety-in-numbers philosophy has everyone buying tulip bulbs along with everyone else, so we'll all lose our shirts together. There is another saying about by the time the vast hordes have latched onto an investment opportunity, it is already too late. There is the Lemmings and a cliff story. Remember what your mother told you: "Suppose everyone else is jumping off a bridge?" You will read further about safety in numbers in a previous publication.

How many people say they just love what they are doing and get drunk-as-a-skunk at lunch and every night? Maybe they just love what they are doing, and they love doing it while drunk-as-a-skunk too, but there are doubts. (*Skunks don't get drunk, nor do they run too fast. Why would they have to run, when all they have to do is raise their tail? They may look drunk, but maybe it just rhymes.*)

One night while they were being walked, one of my rescue doGs literally ran right by a black cat standing there, complete with arched back. The doG normally would have given chase, and the cat would have run away. Any other color cat would have run quickly away and dove in a dumpster for cover. The doG must have thought it was a skunk, so he knew better than to chase it.

So they are trying to force everybody into admitting they are doing what they love, by advertising for people that want to do what they love. Presumably, then, you will be doing what you love. How many people just love standing on their feet all day restocking shelves? Maybe some do, but most don't. Go out for lunch, and get drunk-as-a-skunk, then come back and restock shelves.

The test is: NOT answering an ad to "Do What You Love," but you would not only do whatever for free, but actually *pay* to do it. The easiest examples would be sports: whapping at a ball in a batting cage with a bat, or whapping a tennis ball a machine throws at you. Some pay to do it, while most quickly tire of the whapping "exercise."

The best examples would not just be in a batting cage, or on a tennis court, but would be playing "for free" somewhere, somehow, every day-and-night, rain-or-shine. They would be playing even if they were not playing for free and had to pay.

Many say they love to play golf, but the best not only play for free, but get paid to do it. The same with the best musicians, NFL players, etc. That is doing something you love instead of doing what our parents might have forced upon us at a very early age, *because parents are the ones that might get paid in houses.*

It's easy to look "from the outside" at someone doing what a parent wished they had always done. Most of these are doing what their parents direct them to do, which may or may-not be what a parent wished they had always done, but the child is under a parent's direction none-the-less. Sometimes a parent, with the best of intentions, sets their offspring up in the "family business."

They set the child up in a wonderful business and a terrible *Life*. It was the parent who established the business-they-always-wanted for the child, although in this case, the parent actually wanted it, and left it to the offspring who wanted nothing to do with it. The child just wants to manage his or her own *Life*.

One of my favorite examples is the successful law firm the father leaves to the son after encouraging him to become a lawyer. Let's say the kid always wanted to write, but he's miserable about becoming a lawyer. Do you think the father really wanted to bestow misery on the son? Some parents might, as in the "give back" to the children philosophy. Give them what they did to you.

Stories abound about people leaving the law their parents always wanted them to do, but instead the child is happy doing something else. Law is only one example, but a good one!

Free advice is worth every penny you spend for it: so spend some of those worthless pennies and sell the business to someone who actually *wants* to do it, and go for what you actually *want* to do for free (or pay-to-do-it if necessary). In that manner you will *not* be the same as everybody else; at least you won't be the same as the vast majority doing life from beliefs established from the outside.

Maybe you will write about the experience, and maybe writing is what I always wanted to do. Nobody is paying me by-the-hour to do it, so I guess I AM paying to do it! *Whap!*

YOU'VE BEEN SCAMMED

There is absolutely no intention of converting, or un-converting, anyone to or from anything. Leave that to the Mooney's at the airport and their tambourines. By the definition of Creationism, everyone creates what they believe, via whatever they are doing.

Let it be said you want to know the truth with a capital "T," and if that is what you want, you need seek no further. If you like pancake breakfasts and spaghetti dinners, keep going to them! There's nothing to say you can't have both truth and meals.

There was a time in this country we had what later became known as "patent medicines." Each and every one of them claimed to be able to cure what ailed you. In reality, the medicine contained some derivative of cocaine that honestly might have made you feel better.

Along came the pre-cursor of the FDA, with their truth in labelling requirements, and patent medicines went quickly away. Remember: time (as in quickly) is a creation of the left-brain that also uses words, reasoning, and logic.

There are many people knowingly selling something they know will do little for anyone, but might make them rich in the process. Others might then climb on board *that* wealth express. Does having wealth come from the outside or the inside? Usually it comes from the outside, which is why wealth quickly goes away, and does not make you feel good. But wealth is in society's capitalist model, and coming from the outside, also drives models based on what someone or something else says to do.

There are a bunch of totally reputable people, whom yesterday I would have quickly judged as just plain WRONG, but are willing to convert you to their way of thinking before they retire behind locked gates, with pensions you pay for. They are scam artists, possibly without even knowing it, like politicians or religious leaders can be.

Unfortunately, most politicians or religious leaders are coming from the outside, doing what somebody else told them to do, or they're "modeling" someone else's behavior. They might also be the "religious right" aka bible-thumpers modeling "Christian" behavior.

While they are busy thumping their bible, they are also busy judging you as *WRONG* (which automatically makes them right). Not only are they judging you as wrong, they are also coming from the outside. There is nothing inherently wrong about *classifying* anyone as wrong, but coming from the outside is wrong when you create your *Reality*.

Suggestion: "outsiders" need to come from the inside, and switch their place on their very own *Roadmap-of-Life*, but it's entirely up to them. Alternatives appear once you have switched your place, and you can thereby create your very own *Reality*. Everyone else can go fix yourself (in your computer, by turning on automatic updates).

Are you offended yet? When my cousin's wife tried to "fix-me-up" with her friend without anyone knowing, a *"**Close Encounter of the Third Kind**"* was generated. BTW, in this process I was totally offended and missed some sleep, but I didn't mind being RIGHT.

What you are going to have to do is the same thing I had to do earlier at fix-up time. Stop being so offended and release what needs to be released. At that point you can go about consciously changing where you are on your very own *Roadmap-of-Life*, and can thereby form your beliefs from the inside.

Everything in the fixer-upper incident was coming from the "outside," and that includes my cousin's wife (the fixer-upper). More importantly, having everything coming from the inside (as in creating your own beliefs and thereby your own *Reality*), would be what Creationism teaches.

To reiterate, no-one is trying to convert anyone to anything, because an airport and tambourines would need to be involved. If you really enjoy pancake breakfasts and spaghetti dinners with your tribe, continue going! It's important, though, people are given a different opportunity to find out how things really work if you aren't too offended.

ARE YOU SITTING DOWN?

It should be relatively easy to determine whether you are on the side of *Life* happening to you (your beliefs originate from the outside), or whether you are the cause (your beliefs come to you from the inside). Those are the only two choices, and the results may seem the same, but they're not. Remember the 100-Year rule. Make sure you are NOT deciding that *changing* your choice will be easy, like stopping smoking. *An old joke comes to mind: "It's EASY to stop smoking. I've done it dozens of times!"*

A choice may not be easy to change, but it should be relatively easy to determine whether a behavior is coming from the outside or the inside. Alas, many suggested outside behaviors come from the realm of "do as I say, not as I do" because many are doing what their parents (someone else, a religion, a TV infomercial, or a well-wisher) suggest. By definition advice always – that's *always* – originates outside yourself.

Many are doing, and passing down, what their parents passed down to them. *Sins of the Father, and all that. Life* is happening *to* them from the outside; they are NOT the cause of whatever they believe. Also remember: your belief is what is in the driver's seat.

A belief itself originates from the outside or the inside. Once a belief is there, it always produces results from your interior, even if the belief that puts you where you are, originated outside. It's our job to consciously change places on our roadmap. If we change our place on our very own *Roadmap-of-Life*, our beliefs now originate from the inside (with the possible exception of those items you couldn't change if you tried, like gravity).

Sometimes someone (or something, like a program or a TV infomercial) will make a suggestion to you that seems good at the time. You may even follow it for a while, but ultimately drop it because, as you are learning, it forms a belief which originated outside yourself. You probably feel rotten.

After the suggestion is dropped, a while later it may recur, seemingly all by itself. That's the first hint that this might be a change-in-places on your *Roadmap-of-Life*, where beliefs originate from the inside. The key is: you haven't thought about it, which is in the realm of words, logic, and reason (left-brain) instead of (right-brain) imagination. In Step Two, imagination is where you want to stay while you keep feeling good.

The suggestion is effortlessly followed until you have changed places on your *Roadmap-of-Life*. Only you can determine whether the suggestion (which later turned into a belief, as in "I *believe* I can do *that*") came from the outside, or it originated inside. If you have really changed roadmap places, while at the same time you get a good feeling, chances are good the change was re-introduced from the inside.

If you feel good about having a clean house, not just because your mother said so, you have probably changed positions – BUT – if you grudgingly clean house, you are probably following your mother's instruction which comes from the outside. *Do as I say...*

If you are on the side of *Life* happening to you, you are following the instructions your parents, or maybe a late-night infomercial, handed down or you purchased. Nothing is FREE, as in the proverbial FREE lunch! *Have you learned that lesson yet?*

(*You can flip real-estate using someone else's money. But you must CALL NOW to reserve your FREE spot. Be one of the first ten callers to get a FREE information packet.*) These instructions originate outside yourself for *FREE*.

If the instructions come from inside yourself, you are the cause of your own beliefs about *Reality*. Be careful though, because sometimes the instructions are so innate they will *seem* to come from the inside. It should not be too hard, thinking back, on whether or not you were *told* (took someone's advice) to do this, that, or the other thing. Advice others give, especially the free kind, always originates outside yourself.

Alternatively, an idea comes from inspiration when you are living "in spirit." You will feel good doing what came to you from the inside, but feel bad when *Life* is happening to you. You are doing what somebody else suggests or wants you to do. By definition, advice always comes from outside yourself, especially the "free" kind. As said repetitively, "Free advice is worth every penny you spend for it."

Society says you need to make a lot of money to "give back" to the Government in taxes, which politicians can then spend to achieve their goals, which they have probably gotten from outside themselves. If you make a lot of money, you might feel good or you might be miserable, as has been discussed. You can thank yourself if you feel miserable with or without MONEY; you can also feel good with or without MONEY. Remember: the idea is to keep feeling good.

If you make a lot of money and can feel good, you are probably one of the rarified few that can make a lot of MONEY $$$ and still do what you Love – talented sports figures or musicians come quickly to mind. But there may be times when doing what you Love can still be a bummer, especially if you have done it long enough. Remember: doing anything can be work, which is why we have a left-brain inspired word for it: WORK. If you lose yourself in it and time passes unbeknownst, it is probably not the standard definition of work. The goal remains to be happy.

Being happy is what it is all about, and money is secondary. They say happiness is easier WITH money than WITHOUT it; but there are people WITH money who are still miserable, maybe because of the money: somebody might steal it or tax it. There are plenty of happy people with no money whatsoever ... that is why MONEY is such a catch-22. *Do you know what a "catch-22" is? The "oldsters" might know, even if "young-uns" know the expression!*

A saying says it all. At the end of your life – one second left – you can now engage with the proverbial life review. The saying goes: add up all the happy moments, and that's how happy your life has been. That doesn't sound all that hard or take up all your remaining energy – you've only got one second left anyway!

In the following analogy, we assume the child is an only child; this automatically eliminates the blowing-apart factor that many families experience, after the remaining parent leaves what would seem to some as a trifling amount to two or more heirs (to say nothing of a successful business). I'm sure the parents wanted their children never to speak to one another again!

Notice how many people are extremely miserable doing what their parents said to do, or even running a successful business a parent left them, even if the person rationalizes they are happy. Note the rationalize part. The left-brain "thinks" via logic and reason and requires words. That's how you rationalize.

Let's take an innocuous example of becoming a plumber. If you become a plumber because your father told you it was what he did, he was in a good union, and worked for or even owns his business in the industry, it's not too hard to figure out your direction is coming from the outside: *Life* is happening *to* you. If he owns a business, it's on the verge of becoming a "family business."

You're probably miserable as a plumber, and drink heavily at night to alleviate the stress. But suppose you thought of the idea on your own, and no-one else you know ever considered becoming a plumber.

If becoming a plumber *feels* bad, the incentive might be coming from the outside like: "I need to make a living. Everybody says this would be an easy way!" The key is: "Everybody says..." When everybody says something, you can rest assured any belief comes from the outside. "Free advice is worth every penny you spend for it" is said once again; lots of people hand out free advice.

Figuring it out comes from the rational side of your brain, but nobody on a late-night infomercial you turned to was selling the idea of going to plumber's school, so the idea must have come from inside, right? Does it *feel* good? That's the easy part. Perhaps there's some invention "waiting in the wings" for a new valve or whatever you imagine a plumber might invent.

Are you sitting down for this, because you need to be (not on the throne, as you might anticipate)! Your *Life* is a complete and accurate reflection of the beliefs you have going on in your head. To put it another way, everything you are experiencing was either programmed by your parents or caregivers, or else it was put there by you. This cannot be emphasized enough. The thought, however it got there, is now a programmed belief and creates your *Reality*.

Nobody can answer how, but maybe the why part (about how something happens) can be answered: so you can experience whatever is going on in your head (mostly unconsciously) as "real." Why else would it happen that way? Some kind of cruel joke?

It's what happens when invisible *Infinite* possibilities merges with likewise invisible *Infinite* energy. Einstein said you can neither create nor destroy energy, but it can change form. The merger creates the visible *Reality* of the idea you can eat, sit on, play with, or whatever you do with what you created.

Now that the idea is physical, science can grab ahold of it for manipulation; you can bake a pie and eat it, or make a chair and sit on it, science predicts. An idea has moved from *Infinity* into *Reality*, like the Wright brothers moved flight from an idea into *Reality* at Kitty Hawk. Now *Life* takes over and decides what is real, and what remains an idea.

There you are at the end of your life, ready to turn over the reins of the family law business you were left with, or otherwise retire. Only one itsy-bitsy problem: the son doesn't want the business. It won't take any rain to wash the spider out (even the *idea* of being a lawyer will wash the itsy-bitsy spider out), nor will it climb back up. The son just doesn't want to be a lawyer.

Speaking of spiders, let's take a quick trip in reverse to the animal kingdom and insects. Who do you think taught little Sammy Spider to roll his kill up in a ball and save it for later? While little Sammy doesn't have a choice, you do, and it can be a different choice from now on. Consciously positioning yourself to a new spot on your *Roadmap-of-Life* would be a different choice.

It's easy to blame somebody else that gave you what you now see as bad advice. But who made the decision to take the advice originally? Blaming somebody else is easy, but be advised it also makes you a victim to the extent you followed their advice, and are now blaming them for the bad advice you followed. You get to be a victim to the extent you do not claim complete responsibility for everything in your *Life*.

"OK, OK, OK" you say doing your best Joe Pesci (in the Lethal Weapon movie-series) imitation. "But at least I am not responsible for the economy and getting laid off" you say, adjusting your hat, folding your arms, while feeling vindicated. But there are plenty of people that are doing quite well, regardless of the economy. Whose economic policies do you support anyway? This includes jobs, relationships, colors, and what were previously thought of as coincidences, and the list goes on and on. The list includes everything – and that's *everything* – period.

I had a couple deaths hit me hard as I was writing. They could have stopped me in my tracks. A childhood friend passed on, to be followed a short time later by one of my rescue doGs. The "bad things happen in threes" rule may never happen, and both shoes have already dropped.

These are a couple outside rules someone has. What occurred to me was that NONE OF US was here 100 years ago, nor will be here in another 100. I continued to cogitate on this concept until it turned into my "100-Year rule." It seems to work well.

I was not only sitting down, but literally laying down when the full realization hit me. I hadn't yet "gotten up." The realization was both exciting and scary at the same time, kind of like a roller coaster. Well, *Life* is like a roller coaster, but the goal is to make *Life* resemble the uphill climb on the old-fashioned wooden roller coaster. You know it's going to be fun and scary, but you're safe for now. *Don't be scared until you go over the top in* Life *as well!*

In fact, you're going to be safe at the end too! Unless there is a power failure and you fall out of the roller-coaster when you are upside-down, but how often does that happen? At least you'll be on the NEWS for everyone else to gape at. If there wasn't the chance death would happen, would it be fun anyway? That's why there are roller-coasters and wars!

After all, who among us was here 100 years ago, and who is going to be here in another 100 years? A saying comes to mind: "Nobody gets out of *Life* alive!" So much fun!

OK Boys and Girls, now we get to the meat of the matter. Presumably the pudding is what you really want:

> *How can you have any pudding if you don't eat yer meat?*
> **Another Brick in the Wall; Pink Floyd**

First you have to eat yer meat!

OPINIONS

Many have heard the phrase: "You are entitled to your own opinion. What you are NOT entitled to is your own set of facts." Inherent in this statement is while my opinion may be different than yours, facts always remain the same whomever observes them.

We will start by sweeping the table clean, and remove all the facts and opinions about them. It's really not that hard, and we can start fresh with some facts, common to all. We will put some facts and opinions back individually, and get a handle on which-is-which.

We begin with: whenever left- or right-brain is mentioned, it is for a right-handed person – a left-handed person is the opposite. That can be our first fact which will never change. *Who thought left and right up? Weren't they originally port and starboard? Labels.*

The right-brain is "older" (if you want to include time) and "thinks" an in entirely different way – emotion – than the logical, rational left-brain which thinks in words. I "know" there is a left- and right-brain, because you can actually see light in-between them, predicated on someone's brain which someone took out of a box on the TED stage. It was complete with a spinal column hanging from it – disgusting.

From the on-stage TED brain box, I thereby "know" the fact there are not only right- and left- physical brains, but different consciousness as well. That seems to be a fact.

Consciousness entities are moving into and out of *Infinity* and *Reality* predicated on something observed on a daily basis – people get born and die. That's *Life* (or the lack thereof). This also seems to be a fact.

This is confirmed by great thinkers like Einstein, saying energy can neither be created nor destroyed, but can only change form. Energy itself is right-brain, and as such is more coarse than *Life* energy. Consciousness entities are more refined and personal, and we can thereby use left-brain reason, logic, and words when discussing them.

Throwing time into the mix, it is "time" to mention the newer left-brain, if it is indeed newer. Words, logic, and reasoning are added to our right-brain thinking, and emotion gets subsequently alluded to.

Our left-brain supplies the words from the previously word-less *Infinity*. The words expressed in *The New Oxford Dictionary* are newer than our mind, right? This process gives us left-brain thinking applied to the right-brain, but here we move perilously close to opinion. So let's go back and just stick with the facts. "Just the facts, ma'am" was said on some old-time cop show.

The fact is, we all have two functions of our brain, as evidenced by the two kinds of "thinking," wherever they occur. The right side "thinks" via emotion, and can only be alluded to by words; our left-brain thinks via words, logic, and reason with time added as an offshoot. The right-brain is given to be our creative aspect, and create it did.

Look at all we have created. There are too many examples to list. So the two different kinds of thinking are given as fact. As mentioned, creation gets close to being an opinion; you may be of the opinion that the left-brain is the creative part, and you would thereby be 180-degrees different than most opinions, but the fact remains we have two different kinds of thinking going on.

We all have right-brain stuff going on, but here we have chosen to limit our right-brain thinking about unbounded consciousness, to left-brain consciousness entities we have branded as human. So we start by realizing that as our descent (using Christian terminology) moves from *Infinity* into *Reality* via *Life*, we move from right-brain into left-brain thinking. I don't know any other way to move from fact into something close to opinion, but let's consider *Reality* and *Life* as facts also, along with the previously discussed fact of *Infinity*.

Abraham (more than one invisible consciousness entity) was asked what the "facts" are regarding basic existence. He (they) responded by suggesting the questioner is looking for answers like: 3D space and gravity. These are *agreements* we share concerning our *Reality*, and are NOT unchanging facts shared among *ALL Realities*. According to Abraham, the unchanging facts in *ALL Realities* are:
  1) The Law of Attraction
  2) The Science of Deliberate Creation, and
  3) The Art of Allowing

Notice how agreements cross the boundary between right- and left-brain "facts," even when they are more like opinions. BTW, my left-brain "understanding" is: up and down used to be reversed, in Christian terms. When you pressed the <DOWN> button in your elevator-of-life, you would be headed toward a heaven contained *within* the earth, and not the opposite. But that is clearly just opinion.

Other opinions which may or may not be facts are: as our consciousness entity descends into *Reality* and *Life* from unbounded consciousness and *Infinity*, added are our senses of sight, sound, smell, taste and touch, as well as emotions.

Another fact / opinion is: we get more of what we concentrate on, as well as all the rest of our thinking. Our thinking comes from both sides of our brain, and gets reflected back to us as *Reality*. Then we have our lessons presented to us, which we can learn from or not, before the fact that our consciousness entity goes back to *Infinity* itself; we have thereby completed the circle of *Life*.

> *And the seasons, they go round and round. The painted ponies go up and down*
> > *We're captured on the carousel of time*
> *We can't return, we can only look behind from where we came,*
> *and go round and round in the circle game*
> **Joni Mitchell; *The Circle Game***

In this section are facts like the circle of *Life*, but also presented are opinions, which may or may not be facts – there is no other way to present these. I'll leave it up to you to argue whether they are opinion, or fact. There's not all that many, nor are they very hard to understand in our delightfully left-brain way.

There is one "fact" Creationism agrees on, as well as many others presented here. We create our own *Reality* from our beliefs; such is the long-and-short of Creationism. How about "It is done to you predicated on what you believe [SIC]." Whether this is fact or just opinion, well, you be the judge. Psst: it's a fact.

DON'T ATTACH ANY SIGNIFICANCE

Right now we are at a point where we can change things; the wake is no longer steering the boat. There are whole philosophies that state: live in the *now*, since *now* is the only point where we can actually make and effect decisions. Not yesterday. Not tomorrow. *Now.* [11] A word of caution is in order: it took you a whole *Life* to get this way. You are not going to change everything right now, but you can work on the changes you will make later. It is NOT an excuse to do nothing.

Now *is* the point of power, and now is the only time you can make a decision and take action effecting a change tomorrow. This will become your position on your roadmap tomorrow. Like the map, you are not going to get instantly to Chicago if you are currently in PA, but at least you know exactly where you are, and can start driving! The wake is done steering your boat.

The founder of Religious Science said many times "turn completely away from your results" and said so in many different ways. He may have made the instruction to turn completely away from your *problems*, because you will only get more of the same.

---

[11] Tolle, Eckhart. The Power of Now: A Guide to Spiritual Enlightenment (all pages). New World Library. Kindle Edition.

What he meant was: if we get results we don't like, completely ignore them. When we create our own *Reality*, that is the only choice we have: to ignore our results, or spend time concentrating on them. When you concentrate on results, you get more of them, so worrying about your *Life* is the same as concentrating on problems. Ignore your results or spend more time focused on them: such is completely congruous with moving into beliefs and *Reality* via *Life*, where you get more of what you concentrate on.

Let's say I am tired of: being overweight, a smoker, and biting my nails. I can be an overweight, nail-biting smoker AND be tired too! If I worry about it, such will be my *Reality*. Ooh, I forgot about being drunk. But that's good, right? *I've already changed part of the equation by ignoring it!*

In creating our *Reality*, our choice is to either ignore results and ultimately get something different, or get more of the same. Such is the gist of the "Change Your Mind ... Change Your Life" Religious Science motto. Then you proceed with changing your mind instead of looking at the results you have always gotten.

You can either: 1) purchase a program or ask somebody what to do (the approach taken by most) OR 2) consciously choose to be somewhere else (the approach taken here) on your very own, unique, *Roadmap-of-Life*. Such a roadmap and narrative is a Step One belief which can be changed into a Step Two belief by simply changing the place on your roadmap. Beliefs then come from inside, and create your *Reality*. So says Creationism.

When first starting to be aware of results, I also became aware someone, somewhere, was creating my *Reality* ... *it was me!* I have created my very own *Reality*. Here's the fun part: blaming good-for-nothing results can go to my parents or somebody else following approach #1. But by using approach #2, I have nobody to blame but myself PLUS the results are better and I AM happier. What to do is: turn completely away from already achieved results, which doesn't blame anyone.

You CAN Get There from here!

STEP ONE: DETERMINE EXACTLY WHERE YOU ARE

It took me a long time to drop the "Really?" question, when I was moving from: "It can't really be like that, can it?" to: "Well, if you say so, it must be like that." And it also took a really long time for things to happen – seemingly forever. I could catch the "Well, if you say so …" statement coming up for a long, long time. You might now better understand how things taking forever is on my *Roadmap-of-Life*.

You can readily see the second statement is not all that convincing either. There's the "if you say so," but many will move quickly to consciously thinking that your beliefs create your *Reality*, but not me, apparently. That is a goal for all of us, changing your position on your very own *Roadmap-of-Life*, and things taking forever is not a planned addition to my Step Two.

There may be a whole lot of stuff that comes up when you start noting what is wrong with your *Life* right now, just don't worry or attach any significance to what is wrong, unless you want more of the same. Turn completely away from undesirable outcomes (prioritizing stuff happens later).

The fact is: there WILL BE a whole lot of things that are served up from the left-side of your brain when you are on a right-brain path involving your *Roadmap-of-Life*. I had several conditions all happening simultaneously as I almost literally whirled around saying "I know this is all caused by me. Now what do I need to do to make it different?" before I went back to solving one condition at-a-time. Typical man – solving things.

A *Roadmap-of-Life* showing where I AM is in order, especially the narrative that creates my current *Reality*. But men never, ever stop to ask for directions (do they?) Maybe my direction would be to turn completely away from my results.

You start with any map by knowing exactly where you are. If you are a man, you must also actually look at the map, or else of what use would a map be, even if you know the state you're in? If you know you are in PA, are you in Philadelphia, Pittsburgh, or somewhere else? The best you can do is turn to the Pennsylvania page. You start by knowing exactly where you are.

At least that is how you get started in our example, being in a world governed by maps. In the real world you would not care how you got here, but only need to know where you want to go. Who cares how you got here?

But "how" solutions are provided by *Infinity* and *Reality* in the past too, right? But we still don't care how we got here. *Does anyone look at a map to determine how they got where they are? Some keep looking backwards.*

We start by determining exactly where we are, starting with a spreadsheet (or any other method) and detail the plusses and minuses of your *Life* right now. This will probably be extremely personal, so you might want to clear out anyone from the room (with the exception of your doG, who probably won't tell anyone, and has watched you getting undressed anyway). *DoGs are never embarrassed for you, even if you might be embarrassed by anyone else watching.*

I have included some of: the Step One (before), and Step Two (after) spreadsheets and scripts I used as examples, with most of the private details omitted. My doG wasn't embarrassed for me at all; *since he is asleep, we'll just let him lie.*

I have both plusses and minuses in my spreadsheet detailing where I AM, but I will leave it up to you which comes first on your spreadsheet. There WILL BE some plusses in everyone's *Life*, and I AM yelling this. Although your *Life* may SEEM really terrible, there will be some plusses, even if minor. Plusses will show up, and you should note them (minuses help).

The old adage goes: I have some good NEWS and I have some bad NEWS … which do you want first? I'm not even going to justify my statement by saying "unless your *Life* is really terrible, then you have only bad NEWS." Sorry, but your *Life* is not just bad NEWS, no matter how it seems. Prioritize plusses for later.

You will want to keep your binder or spreadsheet open during this process. For me, *Life* just seems to keep getting worse, bringing up some long-ago memories where I read this short story; what the title was or how long ago it written was has long-since been forgotten, but the story is still there.

The short story went something like: A fellow is going on vacation as his plane passes through a severe storm with turbulence, lightning, etc. He gets to his hotel and is ushered to his room, even though the electricity is out. Accordingly the air-conditioning is out, but it is not hot yet. As the refrigeration is also out, there goes the nice dinner he was planning. Things just keep getting worse. Finally he figures out as his plane passed through the severe storm, the plane had actually crashed and he had died and gone to hell. In Christian terminology, he went to "H*E*double-hockey-sticks." I probably read this in my Christian days, but hell is still apparently a belief in operation in my brain.

The vacation short-story is now front-and-center of my attention. I read it a long time ago, but it is still there. Many, many other stories I have read are long gone and forgotten.

The important point is: the story is STILL in my brain, while my *Life* just seems to keep getting worse. An important point: we create our own hell right here and right now, so I'll log another minus (or is being aware of the story a plus?) and continue.

It may take a while to release old beliefs you may have been raised on, or you were programmed with. Accordingly, it took me a while to move through these long gone (but still in operation) old beliefs not visited for years, especially previously rejected ones. Next *Life* will be better, but who wants to wait that long?

By-the-way, current understanding has it Catholics are now cancelling hell. Just wondering what happens to everyone who is already there? Just let 'em out, like you would do if hell was overcrowded like a prison. They can easily find a job in Washington DC. *The current Catholic politicians are breathing easier.*

Einstein said "Work on one thing at a time." With that in mind, we can prioritize the items (plusses and minuses) from Step One and work on the most critical, as opposed to working on them all, assuring nothing will get done. You might note my belief (things take forever).

It is interesting as one item progresses, others will improve also, even if you do nothing about the latter. This might mean they are related by synchronicity, but that is not an excuse to do nothing. Some will just go away seemingly on their own.

It would take one item being severely out-of-whack to work on one-at-a-time. It was clear I had previously done a lot of mental work on the "political" and "economics" points, but maybe not of the right kind. This might help to explain why things just seem to keep getting worse, along with the short-story still in operation. Even so, I no longer watch what someone else decides to serve up to me as NEWS, nor are "brain-washed" by political podcasts. I think that's better.

Doing mental work on something does not make it better, especially if one does not set out with the intention to make anything better. No-one can explain how these things will work out, but you can change your position on your *Roadmap-of-Life* to a place where things are actually better.

Prioritizing things on your spreadsheet within your plusses and minuses may affect your script. Now comes a fun part, but it should ALL be fun. Write a movie script or something similar to a short story for your *Life* now. Have fun with it. If *Life* isn't fun, then what's the use? This would be done in conjunction with looking at your spreadsheet, or whatever you used to log your entries, detailing the plusses and minuses of your existence.

My most personal items are deleted for this writing, and left are only the most important points as examples. I have included some items that were never an issue for me, but have included them for illustration value. Some of your spreadsheet points may not matter for your story. Looking solely at the items rated with the highest priority, might indicate how your narrative will develop.

Things may seem absolutely NUTS at first, as you move priorities higher and lower, but they will settle in. You are creating a story about the dialog you had with yourself to bring yourself to this point. It is important to note that bringing yourself to this point does not involve anything about getting here (that would be like the wake still steering the boat).

This review only acknowledges being here (maybe you have stayed for a while), like living in a house with a dirt floor; it is not important to know how you got there. Maybe you stayed living in your parents' home – who cares? The wake is no longer steering the boat, and now we are learning how to consciously move to someplace without a dirt floor.

In Step Two, you will also ultimately write a script, narrative, or story about *only* the positives in your desired location. Why would you want to list any negatives where you *want* to be? It is important to only write about the positives and forget about any negatives. You must really, really, want to forget about any negatives regarding where you want to be. You not only want to forget, but you have already forgotten, what? *I forget!*

You CAN Get There from here!

Step1.xlsx

<u>What</u>	<u>Memo</u>
Plusses	
When I need $$$, it is there	But not ***until*** I ***need*** the $$$ (no XTRA $$$)
The belief has always been there	
NOT judgmental in a normal sense	
But apparently I AM in other ways	
Much SOM education, reading, etc.	
Spirituality CREATES my Reality	Working toward this
House maintenance	
Get rid of the yammerer, Sam	
Grass cutting	Done by Sam (for some time)
New roof	Completely ON
Minuses	
Mother raised me	Depression-era thinking
Very Cynical	
At least re: names	Could be from 7th grade teacher?
Allergy symptoms	Runny eyes, nose; while eating?
Ubiquitous	Present always - almost unnoticeable
Facial blemishes	Ubiquitous
Things reflect *everybody else's* priorities	Things take forever
I am a perfectionist – sort of	Shouldn't things be perfect and complete?
People steal shit off me	
Daily maintenance down	Other stuff
Shower, shave	
Sink full of dishes … sometimes	
Economics & Politics	
Listening to podcasts too much	Or am I?

Depressing	What about lying politicians isn't?
House maintenance down	
DO worst	
Overweight	Over optimal 190#
Doctor says asthma will be back	western medicine ...
Doing computer crap	
Access programming	
Out of control (almost)	
Have gone to Hell	Living there (via the short-story)

A short note about using a spreadsheet for your log. Use a couple columns and size them appropriately. Click-and-drag or insert / cut-and-paste to prioritize rows. The goal is not to teach spreadsheets here, just enable one method to be used in this step.

Time Saver: if you have gotten this book (via Kindle or whatever) onto your computer, you can select the spreadsheet and "Save As ..." something you would like.

It is also important to note a Memo field was added to jot down notes on an ongoing basis, and a second "what" column (indented under the first) has been added for much the same purpose. We already noted most personal items were deleted (the ultimate spreadsheet and narrative are quite long), as well as adding others for strictly illustration value, leaving only the most important items as a guide for the next step.

Step1.docx

Step 1 – Script

My Life is created by someone else

Beliefs

I was raised / programmed (after my 8th birthday) by a single Mother with depression-era thinking (there isn't enough; save everything; etc.) Drawers with folded up tin-foil and dried out rubber-band balls were encountered.

I have always had this belief about money. I don't know where it came from, but now via different Law of Attraction teachings, I might have an idea at what age it came if I was inclined to investigate. Maybe it wasn't an age per se, but more of a habit. Maybe a little of each. I don't know, nor do I now care.

What I now know is how to reprogram beliefs, should I desire. I remember a time in which it worked before (with me knowing nothing about beliefs), so here I will concentrate on a time when I used Religious Science (SOM) consciously.

I knew what I needed, according to SOM teachings, and had known for a long time. After all, what is the use knowing it when you don't do it? All I had to do was do it – bummer – but I did so anyway. The year was … I don't know. It was around New Years, Jan 1, of whatever year.

What I did know, was I was making very little money, and had, as they say, no prospects. So every morning I sat down and meditated on prosperity. Every morning. I did visualization on unlimited things like: blades-of-grass, leaves-on-trees, stars, suns, galaxies, atoms, molecules, cells, body systems … whatever came to mind. Then I forgot about it for the rest of the day.

I must have changed my beliefs, because by April I had gotten busy to the point I was now forgetting about the meditation. I had gotten busy with something I never could have planned. Never. So it must have come from somewhere without reason, like *Infinity* is supposed to. Now I was getting paid.

In April of the *next* year I was doing my taxes. I hadn't really gotten underway until May, and I was yet to be paid for Dec of the preceding year, on purpose. So I had about 7 full months of cash income, more-or-less, for the previous year. I had been paying a contact much more than the finder's fee he deserved, but resolving that situation was to come later. Lo-and-behold, I had made almost TWICE what I had made in any previous year, including the errant contact. So I gave a short testimonial about that before a Sun SOM talk, but I was never to talk about it or anything else again, even after asking. Maybe I screwed up, but maybe I was TOO GOOD! Who cares, if it's all about creating my own *Reality*?

Judgment

I am not very judgmental, at least not in the way some people are. The first thing some people see is a person's color, and whether they are fat/skinny, etc. I don't think I have ever been like that. But I will freely admit I will later judge some people on whether-or-not I think they are stupid, but that takes a while; OMG maybe they are just *different* – that I can handle. I also continually opened up to Judgment sections in *Gifts from a Course in Miracles* which was not forgotten.

Playing something

There was a point-in-time in which I was playing both 12-string guitar AND piano. So I played Sun morning service, and Rev Jackie was speaking. I played (**John Denver**) *Annie's Song* on guitar, and (**John Lennon**) *Imagine* on piano: BTW, I think I played too long.

People asked me when I was going to play again. "Simple," I replied. "The next time there is a blue moon on a leap year." The blue moon and leap year are things that really happened, but playing again isn't. I have played very little since, on either instrument, with the exception of the following.

"Lost at Love" (aka Truck driving) was played on guitar at a talent show that featured "The Replacements." JZ, for one, said he loved the song.

If there weren't minuses ...
Let's face it, if your Life didn't have any minuses, you probably wouldn't be reading this. But now that I've covered some of the plusses, let's shift to the minuses. One thing Religious Science taught me was: don't focus on the negative. "You asked for it, you got it" are the lyrics to some commercial.

By-the-by, if I were doing the same thing most everyone else does, I would still be doing what I was born into, and would be Presbyterian. Maybe I would be a JFK DEMocrat. Maybe that's why there are so many DEMocrat Cathloholics, even though that makes absolutely no sense, given DEM abortion beliefs. Making sense of something is only logical left-brain thinking anyway.

Let's admit it; some like pancake breakfasts and spaghetti dinners. There may be some plusses rolled in with this, but that's SOM education for you. One cannot be completely divorced from SOM education undertaken for a long time, and it says you never look at a negative unless followed by a positive.

A persistent problem went almost unnoticed – it was so ubiquitous. My eyes water a lot making seeing hard sometimes, although my eyes are not strained. The running nose comes right along later. As such, they are like allergy symptoms. The running nose gets worse when I am eating, and the tearing eyes get worse when a breeze is blowing, or even when I am going to sleep. Going to sleep is one reason I know there is no eye-strain involved.

It takes a minute for my eyes to start watering and my nose to start running after I wake up. They are usually going strong by the time I get back from my early am dog walk, then they let-up. I used to have the exact opposite eye problem – dry eye – which I attributed to long usage of the computer while not blinking enough. I took some pill or did something to alleviate this problem, which ultimately resulted in the current situation, or so I thought. My nose may have always run when I was eating – I don't remember.

Things seem to take a long time – I mean a really, really long time – like forever. The plus that follows is at least it gets done right! So I'm not expecting writing this script to take a short amount of time, but at least it will be done right. LOL

When I was eight, the same western doctor that killed my father via Big Pharma (and drove me away from western thought) said I would outgrow my childhood wintertime asthma, which I did, after much "work." He also said it would be back later in life, which I continue to recall on occasion. Couple that with being overweight, and I know losing excess # will also nix the return of the asthma, which has been popping up since it has gotten cold. I have been feeling the associated (familiar from childhood) chest-tightness, especially when lying down. I did a little on-line research, and a holistic product showed up. Via check-marks placed alongside symptoms it addressed, I see I had been suffering some symptoms longer.

I recently noted some very poignant negative language around computer "crap." I would never, repeat NEVER, want it to take several hours, or days even, to print something out, or so I fumed. But there it was: taking a really, really long time to print that crap out. I won't bore the reader with the details, but there it was: this BIG STEAMING PILE of computer crap. Suddenly I became aware of how I was being presented with real, live "facts" to match my emotions and narrative – WOW.

I'm really addicted to Spider Solitaire. I used to be addicted to the regular variety of Solitaire, but then I found Spiders. Not the itsy-bitsy kind that get washed out of the rainspout, but the more permanent kind that climbs right-back-up. Thank doG I never stuck any needle in-my-arm, and was too cheap to stick anything up-my-nose and get physically addicted. Addiction would be worse – I could be dead – but would that be all that bad (remember my 100-Year rule)? Who's going to be alive in 100 years to care anyway.

People steal shit off me. Oops, there's a word and some language. What's wrapped up in the word "shit?" The same stuff that's in "computer crap" – unwanted. Flush it down the can and especially from mind. Maybe that's why they stole it from me. It wasn't important and I didn't want it anyway. Then there's the stealing part. The word "steal" itself is very judgmental, and people themselves are, at best, different. But who's *NOT* different from everybody else?

It is extremely important to note that this dialog has been how your *Reality* has been created. That's right, how you talk to yourself is reflected in your *Reality*. It's exactly the same on the outside as it is on the inside. The difference is: on the inside, the mostly unconscious dialog is served up as beliefs. Some philosophies promote stopping the internal dialog entirely, but I don't know what you'd have then.

Remember Einstein said to only work on one thing at a time? I don't think he was talking about the small things (*that* might take forever), but the big things like a new car or home. The small things could fill-in the gaps. One other logical thing: "and" or "or" indicates two goals, even if they work in conjunction with each other. Let the roadmap handle separate goals.

FACTS

Your *Reality* is created by you. Unless you are a victim to someone else, who do you think is creating it? *Psst: You're creating it!* Your very-own, unique *Reality* is created as a reflection of your internal beliefs and habits via your self-dialog, which we have just finished scripting. A fun thing to do at this time would be to see how the script from Step One lines up with your *Life*. Are you having fun yet?

Remember: you can't figure out how such a cross-reference will work. That would be too left-brain logical and rational, and not much fun at all. So we'll just see what's happening, and match it up to your script. You may not *want* to do the "match game," but you *can* match them up, or the situation wouldn't be happening.

Rational, logical thinking just doesn't make it from *Infinity* to *Reality*, or else conversations would go exactly as rehearsed! Starting from right-brain, and going left-brain just doesn't work. When you have imagined a conversation, you would like to think it would start out from someplace on your *Roadmap-of-Life*, like standing up for yourself more in a relationship, job, etc. It might seem like a goal that can be visualized, but goals and visualization are left-brain, logical, *Reality* thinking.

It is even better is to imagine the conversation – imagination comes from your right-brain. *Infinity* "thinking" requires no precedent.

139

Maybe no-one has ever stood up to <whom or whatever> before! Then let the logical, rational, left-brain take over. The conversation will not go as you might have planned, but it may result in things you could never have visualized. For instance, perhaps you get a higher position and raise; the "boss" was just waiting for someone to "step up." Imagine that! Your belief, that "you could do it" was rewarded.

A word to the wise: often what you are doing is so embedded you don't think of it *at all*, you just do it by rote. Having that first cigarette of the day comes to mind. The person just believes, and has been programmed (by themselves) they will die smoking, regardless their parents never smoked. It's a habit picked up later. Remember that first drink or cigarette? Yecch! But now you enjoy not only the first, but every one thereafter! Maybe you don't actually enjoy it as much as you are now in the habit of doing it.

A belief is a thought that becomes automatic and needs to be thought no more. Knowing something is even stronger. In a commercial was this woman who just knew, after she was 30, she would be a smoker all her life. But unbelievably, after using this specific patch (or whatever they were selling) she quit. Not seeing any disclaimers about an actor's portrayal or not trying this at home, it must be true, right? Or does marketing use your own beliefs against you? Taking up smoking would be a good test to see if you could stop! Just kidding. *A current marketing technique declares "Real People ... NOT Actors" which simultaneously declares actors are NOT real people, along with whatever they are selling.*

Several years ago, I got an envelope, where on the outside was "printed" in script: The courtesy of a reply is requested, Mr. Todd. I can still remember thinking "Well isn't that nice!" I can't remember if I replied, but I do think it was opened, which is all the marketers making big bucks want. Several years later, envelopes arrive with the same wording, which is ignored and goes directly, unexamined, into the circular file, along with all the other IMPORTANT and OPEN IMMEDIATELY mail. Does copying someone else give marketers beliefs that ultimately come from the outside, or the inside?

Add things to the list while you are thinking about them. Did you remember to leave the list open? Then prioritize what you do or don't want to get rid of. Much emotion was tied up in my entry of "doing computer crap." Doesn't the word "crap" reveal a lot of feelings? So the Universe perked up its ears and listened. "Good enough" it said. I'll give you more computer crap just so you know I'm listening. So then my hard drive "crapped." *Can't get enough, can you Mr. Universe?*

Earlier, my first hard-drive in this computer was "ticking," and after much research (more "crap!") I found out it was going to go bad. So I went through interminable "crap" backing up and deleting stuff so I could take it to the Computer Store to have the drive replaced. Before I could do so, the computer went through an automatic Windows update, and the drive stopped ticking.

Even though it was now out-of-warranty, I eventually replaced the drive anyway (the second hard-drive had more space, and no ticking!) After the second drive eventually crapped (way before its time) I put the first one back in and tried to boot from it – no luck. Computer crap had now bled over into "things take forever." What a steaming pile of crap.

I needed something printed from a printer I seldom use. Didn't work. A couple days later, after trying everything I could think of, I had determined the printer had crapped. Need I say more? I'm sure somewhere there are people *not* dealing with computer crap and things taking forever – maybe they pay someone else to do it – in any event they are not doing it themselves. What do they say: "Such is *Life?*" Such crap is nowhere in their dialog.

Going to my car in the carport immediately out of my sunroom, something seemed amiss. Perhaps being observant should be under my "plusses." Other items in the car were disturbed. Someone had "stolen my shit."

Among the "stolen shit" were some things that could go away without "thinking" (in a normal / rational way) any more about them; they had become totally useless. I didn't "think" this would happen, after a person who had previously been living here was so sure things were going to get stolen. Now that I look back, it had happened before and would happen again if I did not plan on it NOT happening by making that an aspect of my dialog in Step Two.

Such are some of the facts presented by your *Life*. I am continually amazed by the relation of beliefs and facts. Did not someone once say: "it is done to you predicated on your beliefs?" Would beliefs be internal? Where do they come from?

You CAN Get There from here!

STEP TWO: MOVE
SOMEPLACE DIFFERENT

While moving someplace different on my *Roadmap-of-Life*, a lot of thought was entertained about different ways of journaling; common among them is the use of journaling as a tool for getting in touch (using words) with right-brain *Infinity* that normally does not use words whatsoever. Journaling started to look like a good way to generate a Step Two script about being where I want to be. Something didn't seem just right though, requiring further thinking of the left-brain kind using logic and reason.

The result was: Step Two is in the future – one or more possibilities are turned into probabilities – and consciously moving to that location on your *Roadmap-of-Life* **NOW** (remember: NOW is the "point of power.") *Infinity* shows up with selections, then you use *Life* to make certain choices. Your *Reality* later will reflect these choices, especially if they have been thought enough times to be programmed as beliefs. *Life* is a process that continues on into the future (until it all get rolled back into *Infinity* in 100 years or so), whether you choose to consciously engage with *Life* or not.

Many in today's world journal, but the exercise is more like a diary. At "the end-of-the-day, she wrote down what happened" in her journal (or would that be her diary?) Having a journal sounds so much cooler than a diary; contrast "She locked her diary and stuffed it under her mattress" with the same statement, using 'journal' instead of 'diary.' *Diary is so yesterday it gets done by candlelight.*

Today, she can even keep a journal on her laptop and password protect it from her Mom! Maybe she thinks she is journaling, but it's not the same. Her journaling is done in the past – what happened that day. Happened is past tense. What will happen with Step Two is different, because it's future oriented (at least until you get there, preceded by NOW).

Don't be alarmed if you wish to move someplace physically different. Someplace different is on your *Roadmap-of-Life* (you can't get around that) but it's not necessarily physically different. I AM talking about moving to a different place in your *Life*. You can't stop moving forward in *Life*, but some results are better than others.

You have now determined where you are, and your *Life* sucks pretty bad if you have read this far. Now it's time for you to consciously choose where you want to be. Remember: it is *your* choice, not somebody else's, as if you are a victim to them. You will probably work on this part in conjunction with determining where you are now. You did not get to right here (reading this and working through the examples) by being passive and letting *Life* just happen to you.

But you may be passive and *Life* just happens to you up to now, when you opened this book. No matter how passive you were, at many points a decision was required to go right or left, and you chose the way. No one else made the choice, although it might seem that way. Did your mother or father REALLY force you to go left? Really? Were they sitting in your lap turning the steering-wheel?

Many have made a choice that probably seemed correct at the time. At the very least, you can blame someone else for making the choice, as the driver turns left. Many have died making NO OTHER

CHOICE but to continue hands-off. By default you may go over a cliff, continuing down the same road in the same direction, making no changes.

> *Drivin' with your eyes closed*
> *There's gonna be a crash – everybody knows!*
> **Bruce Hornsby; *The Range***

Maybe a **Road Less Travelled** is really where you want to be. Wherever you are in *Life*, the choice is up to you whether to stay on the same road, going the same way, or not.

Your first step is to write a script for where you are. This can take many different forms as you write your own script, which should turn out to be an accurate reflection of your *Life*, as a mirror is also an accurate reflection.

Things will come to you, helping to clarify your position in *Life*. There are many guides on-line to help with scripts, just pick one. Don't pick any, if that suits you better, just go for a script! Remember: this script doesn't get turned in, and is NOT supposed to be read by anyone else (*but your doG may watch!*)

Then make a list of where you want to be (remember: plusses only are contained in Step Two) and write a movie script for your dialog as you are now completely changed. Name it.

There WILL BE things that come completely from inside yourself, as well as some things that at least started on the outside. Add them to your newer / better beliefs. Hint: making mega money may be one of those things that show up. Such a goal probably comes from the outside and may overshadow others – maybe not. Let's take a closer look.

The ultimate goal is to be happy. At the very last moment of your life, you can add up all the happy moments you have had, and that's how happy a life you have had. There's no other way to look at it. Open your eyes – don't be *Drivin' with your eyes closed!*

There are stories about the miserable person who has MONEY. He sits around counting it all the time, and worries about how much it is going to be taxed and who is going to steal it. He only wishes he could afford to go on the vacation the person who ostensibly has no MONEY is on.

> *Levon, Levon likes his money. He makes a lot they say.*
> *Spends his days counting … in a garage, by the motorway.*
> **Elton John***; Levon*

But the person with no MONEY is happy. You never see them without a smile on their face. So, can you say that MONEY is what makes you happy, or the reverse? There is a saying: It's easier to be happy WITH MONEY than WITHOUT it. True, false, or doesn't matter?

Let's look at a three-generation, but small, southern law firm. Some guy could be very happy writing a book about it (we'll call it *The Firm,* or is it *To Kill a Mockingbird,* or maybe *One Flew over the Cuckoo's Nest*) but that's a whole 'nother story, so to speak. The first generation, in this case the grandfather, studies and practices law, and ultimately hangs out a shingle for a small firm which he calls "Ogelby, ATTORNEY AT LAW." He is reasonably happy.

His son follows in his father's footsteps – it's the way things were done. He goes to law school, becomes a lawyer, and is ready to run the firm when his father chooses to do so no longer. The first generation changes the name of the law firm he founded, and the shingle now reads "Ogelby & Son, ATTORNEYS AT LAW."

You cannot tell if the second generation is happy or not, because the lines on his face don't show it. There is plenty of MONEY (you can tell, because they have Thanksgiving dinner at the grandfather's big house on the hill).

Now the third generation is ready, given his age, to become a lawyer and run the family practice. The grandfather envisions the shingle now reading "Ogelby & Family, ATTORNEYS AT LAW." Drinking is forbidden on Thanksgiving after that one year. But the grandson has other thoughts. He knows he would be miserable doing what his father is grooming him for (it is also a relationship with other problems! *Let's face it – one's the father, the other the son!*)

The grandson does not even try out being miserable for a while, as many have done on a more permanent basis. He goes right to being happy, and chooses something he knows he will be happy doing: writing. He loves writing: fiction, non-fiction, poetry, whatever – he has been doing it all his *Life*.

"But there's no money in writing," his father and grandfather argue with the grandson. Remember what they believe about "The starving artist?" To the grand-father and father, writing is an art.

MONEY $$$ is not everything – happiness is. Can it be said MONEY is their (*or society's*) goal, and this goal comes from the outside? The grandson does not even try law.

Let's use another analogy. Many have heard about not mixing drink with talk, especially about politics or religion, and especially not at the holiday table. We'll make this particular holiday Thanksgiving to keep it secular, and there are two separate, but otherwise identical, cousins with opposite beliefs at the table.

One cousin believes the government is the ANSWER to all problems, where the other has the belief the government IS THE CAUSE of most problems. They obey at least some of the rules and do not discuss politics, or else they would be rolling around the front lawn in a death grip convincing the other he is *RIGHT* and the other is *WRONG*. Now they nurse their Brandy Alexanders in public, but their beliefs are nursed in private.

One watches MSNBC "religiously" while the other listens to Rush Limbaugh. The NEWS shows talk about the same things. Do you see how beliefs work now? Separate but equal. Give Thanks.

You CAN Get There from here!

Step2.xls

| <u>**What**</u> | <u>**Memo**</u> |

plusses

What	Memo
$$$ arrives QUICKLY	become an author and coach
breathing is EASY	Asthma is done!
right and perfect 190# weight	facial blemishes are gone
living in Sitka, AK	coaching; cruise ship lectures
daily maintenance up	other stuff
shower	
dishes	kept to a minimum
cooking	lots of leftovers to heat up
house maintenance	
New Roof ON	
LR Windows FINISHED	
Replace radiant heat w/ baseboard	
Relationship with beautiful 40+ year-old	
I sleep as long as I want	Or am I sleeping thru Life?

Step2.docx

Life is created by ME ! ! !

Step 2 – Script

I no longer engage with Depression-era, nor western thinking AT ALL.

I AM breathing fine, with no trace of any childhood asthma the western MD said would return.

I treat everyone and everything with respect, especially regarding their label (their name the left-brain has assigned).

I used to believe when I needed MONEY it would appear – this belief worked well earlier. Now I AM reprogramming the belief, and getting rid of the part where I *need* MONEY for the belief to work. This time *I know and affirm* financial abundance comes very quickly, whether I need it or not. I AM a published author, coach, and speaker. I have more MONEY than I know what to do with; I AM so successful!

On MONEY $$$ – now there's so much of it I just give it away!

Living in Sitka, AK, my books are being sold locally in book stores in Juneau and on Amazon, etc. I AM a coach; giving on-shipboard lectures about how to re-arrange your *Life* according to Creationism – the "new way." While doing so, I AM on ships going between Sitka and Juneau watching whales, dolphins, and glaciers calving.

I have a relationship with a beautiful, smart and abundant 40-plus year old who doesn't care if she lives in PA, TX, or AK where she takes care of my house when I am away. She is "normal" from a male perspective, and very conservative. I don't need, nor want, to convert her to anything political, philosophical, religious, or anything. Strangely for a female, she does not even want to discuss it, although she talks about lots of other stuff! She is very intelligent.

NOW – I know what I need to do, according to these exercises.

I know I'm a male who, according to popular thinking, never stops to ask for directions (LOL) – but these exercises are different – I can do them under *this* direction. I could play in the NFL if I could only exercise enough! But NOW I don't care.

I authored my first book and it is printed, with boxes of it awaiting <whatever>. My marketing was starting to be in place, beginning with somebody like me speaking about the books. I continue to forget about it.

This is the same as the (last) "release" step taught in Religious Science prayer, in what they term "prayer treatment." This last step is often stated as "And So It Is!"

You CAN Get There from here! – And So It Is ! ! !

BETTER FACTS

You may have noticed your spreadsheet and script for Step Two are noticeably shorter than for Step One, or it is supposed to be that way? As your *Life* gets better and the bad falls away, your *Life* is replaced with the good, and the results from Step Two (especially the narrative) will eventually get longer than Step One, but *only if* you remain keeping track.

To repeat a sentiment expressed many times: your *Reality* is created by you. Who else did you think was doing it? Now that you have changed your location on your very own *Roadmap-of-Life*, things should be looking better.

When originally getting published, there were "roadblocks," many of which are detailed above (Step One has "minuses"), along with a big steaming pile of "computer crap." One of the reasons involved in changing locations on my *Roadmap-of-Life* was to get out from under all that stuff, and be happier!

One of the services was marketing, under the "better mousetrap" theory. Remember the saying "If you build a better mousetrap, the world will beat a path to your door"? Not so, especially if no-one knows about it. I saw marketing as a solution; it's also how marketers make the big bucks, even the ones with cute little sayings on the outside of envelopes.

Making big bucks – that's funny. Oy ve, where does marketing come from? Some philosophies would tell me to be more careful with my thinking coming from beliefs which, in turn, are rather logical. That's where the term "model" comes in, as in "model your behavior after that one." After all the preceding, do you know what kind of thinking (inside or outside) ultimately spawns modeling behavior?

Beliefs are a concept explained and returned to many times over. A belief is defined as a thought that is thought so many times over, it needs to be consciously thought no longer and becomes automatic. A thought, as a belief, can be pushed down to the realm of automatic thinking by many methods that might include: programming by parents, caregivers, or society; habits (generally thought of as "bad") acquired later by yourself; or just-plain repetitive thinking (as in "brainwashing") are among them. Don't forget modeling someone else's behavior.

There is yet another method by which a thought is rendered "automatic," and is more like brainwashing. Instead of thinking something over and over, *read* it over and over. Unless you have found a way to turn your thinking off while reading, you will be thinking it too. Viola! After you have read your Step Two narrative over-and-over again, it will become automatic thinking.

"Thoughts are things" is floating around from somewhere, elegant in its simplicity. And somewhere it also says something about getting what you believe. Abraham and others add something about beliefs working best when you believe you have already received it. Not quite as simple anymore, but being a self-proclaimed master of best practices with important parts included, we'll take it. *Are you offended yet?*

Although publishing a book is an intellectual exercise, it is very similar in certain ways to patenting a physical product. Although many of the details of patenting a physical product have changed, the overall effort stayed with me from wherever I learned it, especially now that I can apply it to publishing.

Someone said they came up with the idea of "The Clapper" (clap on, clap off) first and should be rich, but they just couldn't think of a way that was loud enough, and with you all the time. They must not have believed they could do it (patent it might be added).

Having AN IDEA for a product many consider a reason for getting rich. Having the idea only counts as a "1" (one – NOT unity) on the effort scale, and many will have the same idea around the same time. That's the creativity inherent in the right-brain and *Infinity*. Everybody is always linking in to the *Infinite* and having ideas, and it doesn't count for much: everybody is doing it. All the ideas coming forth from publishing something may be different, but an idea still doesn't count for much.

Making a prototype used to be a necessary step for patenting a physical product, but no more. Apparently you can move directly to the patent step with little more than an idea. In publishing however, a functional prototype might be the equivalent of the first draft of a writing. The effort scale now moves up to a "10."

For patenting, you used to have to manufacture one of <*whatever-it-is*>. For printing, you would need to finish your drafts, find a publisher, and set up to have your work printed. The effort scale has now moved to "100." *That's a one with two zeroes attached, or one times ten-squared for those extremely nerdy.*

When a physical product is involved, you then need to patent, mass-produce, and market it. For a printed work like a book, it would need to be printed and marketed. The effort scale is now at "1,000" and marketing is included. *Move over mice and the mousetrap. My idea is now published, and the world is beating a path to my door!*

Although there are obvious differences between products and writing, the knowledge about filing a patent is similar. How an idea gets published, with benchmarks along the way, are thereby included. The *result* is one such similarity, and the rest are details supported by words and thinking of the left-brain type.

Speaking of marketing, as soon as I considered marketing my book, public speaking showed up from a couple sources, including one that declared "speaking is the new marketing!" Speaking of right-brain thinking, imagine that!

What I really needed to do was change my location on my *Roadmap-of-Life*. I could thereby flip the whole page to another one, become a published author, while at the same time making me happy-er!

You CAN Get There from here!

IN A NUTSHELL

In wrapping up, I intended the nutshell view, like "in a nutshell." Excitement led my day as, upon awakening, the nutshell view was all there, complete in its simplicity. It did take a minute to make sure I was not still dreaming, however. There was this dream once-upon-a-time in which I ostensibly woke up, but was still dreaming, but that's a whole 'nother story. *There was a side-effect listed (advertised?) for some drug: "may cause unusual dreams." They must also sell a pill that gives you normal dreams.*

I mentioned earlier it could all be summed up in a single word which will be given later. Now would be a good time to give that single word, but only if you're ready for it. Psst: the word might be consciousness. Another hint: the word might be beliefs. Since everything contains consciousness, the human brand of belief is contained in the philosophy of Creationism.

Wasn't there a game show on TV sometime in the past where they whispered "The word is:" followed by the word? Something popped up with the word visible only to the player giving the clues. Since they seem to have a problem coming up with new shows, it will shortly be back on in a slightly changed manner by another host (the original host might have re-entered *Infinity*).

Everything is some function of belief, either conscious thought or programmed. But we do need to elaborate on it, so you can understand why we spent all this time and effort coming here ("here" is coming into this *Life*) which would not be just reading this book.

Consciousness in this context does not mean some sort of universal consciousness, nor individual consciousness. It originally comes in a coarse sense from *Infinity*: consciousness is invisible, everywhere, no place that it's not, etc. As you refine it, consciousness passes from Universal, shared, or mass; through the individual level, and down into whatever level trees and rocks have. It thereby goes from right-to-left-brain in the physical, and gets to where it can change your place on your *Roadmap-of-Life*. Consciousness (with all associated beliefs about *Infinity*) may resemble what some refer to as the "G" word, and humans can fight over the word (as well as building chapels and religions to it).

The term "consciousness entity" was introduced, then applied to both sides of the brain. We agreed to limit it here to humanity (and not include indoor and outdoor animals, etc.) so as to keep the discussion contained. The consciousness entity would thereby be human, and you wake up one day as a consciousness entity in a single *Reality*. All people wake up in this manner.

Life comes complete with the three pieces of existence: (invisible) *Infinity*, (visible) *Reality*, with *Life* acting as a referee between the invisible (unformed, all potentials) and the visible (something specific in form). Ideas go back and forth from the invisible to the visible; such is *Life* which acts as the referee (and there are *no other options*). *Life*, true to form, makes things a visible *Reality* as you open your eyes to look around. Perception rules the day!

Deepak Chopra says in his book ***The Future of God***
Perception defines Reality. [12]
What is perception, but it comes from consciousness? The big "G"
word is defined as the "*Infinite*" with "invisible" sometimes thrown
in. When the invisible *Infinite* becomes visible, it also becomes "real"
and is thereby your *Reality*. Your *Reality* is also your *Life*!

Since you already come from *Infinity* where everything is possible,
you can change your location on the multi-dimensional *Roadmap-of-
Life* if you desire. How long changing a location might take depends
solely on you, and how long you believe it will take. When you have
moved to another spot, your perception (which includes your *Reality*
and *Life*) has also changed.

The Seth Material said that organizing multiple consciousnesses,
was like a plant with roots shooting down into multiple centuries.
The fourth century had the consciousness of some Pope in that root,
and the seventeenth century had that root as a mother, etc. Even
though we use "century" as a guidepost, using our *Multi-dimensional
Roadmap* largely eliminates time from the picture.

It also helps explain things like savants who can play concert-type
selections without ever seeing a piano before. They, in some manner,
travel down another root to a "time" when they played concert piano.
One having a highly-developed ability with little or no "practice"
(a logical activity) may share some of these aspects of consciousness
with the savant.

It has been explicitly stated multiple times there is no intention to
convert anyone to or from any beliefs or philosophy you currently
hold dear, and this includes religion and spirituality *et al*. Given

[12] Chopra, Deepak (2014-11-11). The Future of God: A Practical Approach to
Spirituality for Our Times (Kindle Locations 1062-1063). Potter/TenSpeed/
Harmony. Kindle Edition.

the preceding discussion, it may be that philosophies do not evolve through any time line, as much as share insights through common "roots."

Accordingly, many insights come from New Thought Religion, since New Thought explicitly intends to bring religion (right-brain) and science (left-brain) together. When you take my "best practices" approach, then add some "free thinking," now you too can be ISO 9001 Certified!

Using your physical senses helps you navigate the world, and the "emotional sense" helps you communicate with the non-physical world you came from, and know you are creating something of your own choosing; all these senses are provided to you upon attaining *Life*. Just keep feeling "good," according to the Law of Attraction.

The environment reflects back more on the same wavelength so you can know exactly where you stand, and makes our thinking seem "real" on the outside. An important note: if the environment reflects back our inside thinking so you can see it on the outside, how can that happen if you are not creating what you are seeing?

To complete the circle, you might want to add the three laws present in every *Reality* vis-à-vis the Law of Attraction. Then you die (*Life's a Beach and all that*) and go back to where you came from, which is invisible to almost everyone not already there.

The only "mysteries" surround the how and why some things happen. Whenever someone figures out the "how," let me know, but don't try too hard! The "why" is a subject of speculation, and has already been speculated upon; that is literally all there is. Since the three pieces of existence are infinite (yet paradoxically simple), they have the capacity to handle all the details, as well as speculation. That's it!

Along comes *Life* to fill in how details happen, which makes it easier to go from the form-less invisible *Infinite* to in form visible *Reality* and back again. *Life* can work with whatever program has been provided by your parents, society (or late-night infomercials!), yourself, or whatever combination, but feeling good is the only object. If you don't feel good, you're missing something, at least according to the great beyond.

You can see it does not take thousand-and-thousands of pages of special instructions and explanations to accomplish. Remember: our purpose here is not to convert anyone into or out of anything, since every philosophy presumably has some good points, or else it wouldn't be around. Just remember: the Universe could care less!

Follow the good points (or even the bad points) by your own choosing. Later, by left-brain thinking involving time, you might get more good and less bad. The *Infinite* has room for all the details – just keep feeling good!

A previous label for *Life* was the *Power of Creation* (they are the same thing). Creation does, always has, and always will, occur *without* words – in silence. It went on long before any program was written down and sold via some late-night infomercial. Along comes the world of logic and words some call science to share the discussion stage. Yes, science now wants to monopolize the discussion, as religion has done for so, so long.

The "In a Nutshell" view would not be complete without a couple examples of the totally-logical left-brain *Reality* way, to contrast with the way that incorporates only the right-brain *Infinity* that makes things happen. Let's start with an easy example: stopping smoking.

The *Reality* way would have you following the ad you saw on TV (or purchasing some other program), apply the patch, and stick to the schedule. That's the model. At the end, hopefully you would be done smoking, but it probably wouldn't be easy (you might continue to crave cigarettes, and go back to smoking). But at least you are done smoking for now.

The *Infinity* way would have you moving to another place on your multi-dimensional *Roadmap-of-Life*, where you are a healthy non-smoker. To be clear, you might purchase the patch or a program as in the old way, or something else might "show up" (including just stopping smoking) and you would probably be "happy" and never return to cravings again. You are at another point on your very own *Roadmap-of-Life*. Hint: if stopping smoking is important enough to you, it might be part of your program, and be on your Step Two list and in your before-and-after dialog. Afterwards, you are a healthy non-smoker ... for good.

Many have the bumper-sticker "C*O*E*X*I*S*T" on their old Volvo. That's fine, as far as it goes. But nowhere is the word "peacefully," in which peaceful does not exist on cell-block-four, nor in the Middle-East. Forced coexistence is not the same as peaceful. *Just saying.*

A "C*O*E*X*I*S*T" left-brain example would include, by definition, many others (and politics) since many other visible consciousness entities (people) get involved. *Reality* would have you living in a world of violent confrontation, and take whatever action "they" (left-brainers) would suggest to ameliorate it. Perhaps you would join the military, or become a lawyer or politician. As you might have surmised, *Reality* would NOT PROVIDE an easy solution.

Infinity (via Creationism) would have you living in a place of peaceful coexistence on your newer-better *Roadmap-of-Life*. "Peacefully C*O*E*X*I*S*T" would be the bumper-sticker on your new Volvo. Which would you choose?

Maybe words have always been in the physical, hence the outward reflection of what thinking is going on inside (conscious and *un*conscious) which usually includes words – at least it started that way. Some philosophies embrace the "always" concept beyond what we know as time. Thereby every existence is like a root reaching into another time; this would seemingly infer time without words. But that's just words and another philosophy and program. *Get a Life!* LOL (You do know what LOL means by this time, don't you?)

You CAN Get There from here!

Now you're finished reading this, you are qualified to change your position:

- Starting from *Infinity* ...
- Determine exactly where you are on your *Roadmap-of-Life*
- Where do you want to be on your *Roadmap-of-Life*?
- Take the steps to get from where you are, to where you want to be
- ***You CAN Get There*** from here

AFTERWORD

A religion may be based on a previous religion, or it may be some combination of previous thoughts. No-one currently knows (or may ever know) whether your single *Reality* contains links to other *Realities*, with roots shooting into those other *Realities* like a plant, although there may be some evidence for that. Savants (or the links they use) may involve some other kind of evolution. "Thinking" about *that* using words (left-brain) *and* imagination (right-brain) would involve, by definition, both sides of your brain (or both types of thinking). Such is evolution.

Let's say you have something in your *Life* created by a belief you don't like. You ultimately put the belief there, and maintain it. Later, your parents, or someone else, may have offered advice – sometimes requested. Even if they programmed it originally, they do not maintain your belief – you do.

No-one sat on your lap and forced you to make that left turn, even if they previously taught you how to drive. Here's a GOOD kicker: if there is something in your *Life* you DO like, you put it in there too, and now it might be listed under plusses in Step One, or contained in Step Two.

Usually minuses come first as you cogitate (since thinking about your negatives is so much fun *especially when you can blame* don't likes *on somebody else*) but in here plusses come first (Step Two should NEVER contain any minuses).

MONEY is one of those double-edged swords: some don't like it, most do, and some could care less one-way-or-the-other; *maybe it's a triple-edged sword – whatever that is. Have you heard the saying: it's so much easier to like something if you already have MONEY?*

Are you offended yet? Maybe you need to be paid MONEY to be really offended, or you're the type NEVER to be offended. Maybe you need to read this again – at least once – to make sure how doubly or triply offended you really are.

Despite my explicit directions whereby this writing was not intended to convert anyone into or out of anything they already believe, there was a time in which I would NOT assign a term to this philosophy; having no term (or label) for it was in order that no-one could have anything to latch onto (as in "that <previously ungiven name> is a load of crap"). If you like your pancake breakfasts and spaghetti dinners, continue going! *Chances are good they will still be there regardless!*

But I eventually assigned the name of "Creationism" to this philosophy, not just because it is so apropos (as in "Everyone Creates their own *Reality*"), but because it needed a name. If you can show me where any line might be as in "I created this (on this side of the line) but I definitely did NOT create that (on the other side)," be my guest. Just don't try too hard.

A word to the wise: the line is NOT between good stuff and bad stuff, as in "I created the good stuff, but I definitely did NOT create the bad stuff (*my parents did!*)" Somebody else created the bad stuff! *Psst: you created it all!*

Creationism is related to consciously changing to a new position on your individual *Roadmap-of-Life*, whereby you create only good stuff. You create it all (but remember the 100-Year rule) and it's all good!

So now we have a word for our previously unexpressed internal beliefs: "Creationism." It includes no lines such as: everything on *that side* (the PLUS side) I AM responsible for, but the other side (the MINUS side) might indicate: I never created *that*. But you created it all! Such is Creationism.

So where do we go from here? We will move consciously to another place which you have chosen on your *Roadmap-of-Life*. This can happen, but only if you did not choose to take your hands off the wheel and wind up wherever *Life* takes you. Taking your hands off the wheel is a choice too.

Now that you know you create your own *Reality*, you also know what to do.

> *There was a fellow walking through the desert, deep in thought, but otherwise minding his own business. A bolt of lightning struck nearby, setting a bush on fire. He thoughtfully watched it burn for a minute, then exclaimed to anyone who might be listening "But could you be a little more clear?"*

You CAN Get There from here!

SUGGESTIONS FOR READING AND WATCHING

It seems a lot of time might be left over for reading; listed are some suggestions. Additionally, look at footnoted material.

- The Law of Attraction (LOA) Abraham series channeled through Ester Hicks.
  - The book *The Law of Attraction* by Ester and Jerry Hicks gives a good summary of what the law is and how it operates
  - *Ask and It Is Given*: Learning to Manifest Your Desires
  - *Co-creating at its best*
  - *The Astonishing Power of Emotions*
  - www.Abraham-Hicks.com
  - You can get DVDs of actual sessions from their website, or through Netflix
- Deepak Chopra
  - *The Future of God*
- Dr. Sonia Choquette
  - *Tune In: Let Your Intuition Guide You*
- Dr. Joe Dispenza
  - *Breaking the Habit of Being Yourself*
  - *Evolve Your Brain*
- Dr. Wayne W. Dyer

- o Author *et al* of works in many media, including PBS specials
- Jane Roberts channels *The Seth Material*
  - o Especially *The Nature of Personal Reality*
  - o many more books
  - o Look for video of her channeling via YouTube!
- Mike Dooley
  - o *The Top Ten Things Dead People Want to Tell You*
- Napoleon Hill
  - o *Think and Grow Rich* (a classic)
  - o The Abraham series are an offshoot of this classic work
- R Preston Todd
  - o *The Way It Is*
  - o *You didn't think you would get to this point without me hawking my previous book, did you?*

Of course, there are many more too numerous to mention!

GLOSSARY

Here you will find definitions for some terms you may not be familiar with, or might be used in a "non-traditional" manner.

100-Year rule – 100 years previously, or in 100 years hence, no-one on the planet right now will be around *to care*

addict(ed) – to the habit of doing something

advice – always comes from someone else, and from the outside

agreement – a term used to differentiate between: the standard laws used in our *Reality* (many of them), and the "base laws" (3 of them *only* – used in every *Reality*) by the Law of Attraction

Akashic Records –a term started in the late 1800s by Theosophists. The Records are a collection of thoughts, events, and emotions from the astral plane, and are never physical / visible or able to be "proven" (in our terms)

Abraham – a body of channeled knowledge, given by many non-physical consciousness entities, which directly follow the Seth Material and incorporate emotions as well; see Seth

Area 51 – an "off limits" (to mostly everyone) area given to have experienced "unusual" occurrences outside the scope of our *Reality*

astrology – a method of developing a chart for your *Life* based on the date, time, and physical (actual) location of your birth; see numerology

attention – is obtained by placing it with a given intensity on something; see good bad – not acceptable; applied to thinking, beliefs, emotions, or outcomes; obtained by placing your negative attention on something; see good

beginning – the start of things; having no time attached

belief – An interior thought, thought so many times over it becomes a conscious thought no more, and is pushed down into the subconscious where it operates without further attention and is "programmed." When strong enough, it is a "knowing"

bible – the written scripture of Judaism and Christianity; see scripture

brain – the physical organ in the body that is the interface to all the other functions of our body, as well as housing all our memories, programming, and links us to *Infinity*. Left- and right- are reversed in left-handed people (those whose dominant side is their left)

> left- this side of our brain controls the right side of our body. It is finite, also houses our reasoning facility and ego, and "thinks" in words

> right- this side of our brain controls the left side of our body, and our emotions. It is thought to be involved with our creativity. It is also our link to *Infinity*. It "thinks" via emotions with no words whatsoever

> washed - whereby one is exposed to something so much (it does not matter whether it is false) you believe it; see belief

channel(ed) – channeled wisdom comes from a non-physical entity (or entities) in which *Infinity* arrives in words through a person, operating in a trance-like state, who is known as a channel. Sometimes communication can be two ways (i.e. questions can be asked)

change – when a person becomes no longer satisfied with where he or she is, change is required. Here, change involves consciously moving to another place on your *Roadmap-of-Life*

Christianity – a religious philosophy centered on the teachings of Jesus Christ coarse – a property of *Infinity* that is everywhere, nowhere, and invisible – similar to "God" in religion; a collection of (similar) possibilities existing as potentials in a your right-brain, that allows them to be discussed with left-brain words; see possibilities

coincidence – one thing happens at the same time as another, as if by chance

communicate – how we interact with a lot of things. With *Reality*, we use senses and words; with *Infinity*, we use emotions

consciousness – controls everything, including perceptions; it may be right- or left-brain

-entity – a refinement of mass consciousness into individual or personal, in order we might talk about it in a left-brain manner; see consciousness

-mass – an impersonal shared observation

convert – the process of changing a person's inherent beliefs from one philosophy to another

crap – slang that means "bad"

creation – when creation comes from internal beliefs, you may be said to form your own *Reality*

Creationism – a philosophy based on creating your *Reality*; see creation

default – the state in which you take no action (aka doing nothing)

devil – a concept in Christianity that contains all bad; see evil

dialog (self) – the conversation we have with ourselves that determines our Reality

dimension – often used as an equivalent for *Reality*

divine – related to invisible *Infinity*, right-brain, or God

dream – to perceive something while asleep

duality – in order to talk about something perceived using logic and reason, it must exist in the world of duality (hot/cold; up/down, etc.)

Einstein – one of the 20th century's great left-brain thinkers (where thinking occurs using logic)

emotion – an often ignored "sense" used for communicating with
  Infinity

energy – in its coarse form, is invisible and not physical; it can be
  refined into individual forms which we can then talk about
  using words

entity – a personalized conscious occurrence of something which
  otherwise occurs in invisible *Infinity*

eternity – an occurrence of time representing a really, really long
  time

evil – contains nothing but "bad" characteristics; see bad, devil

evolution – the natural process of moving from a lesser to a
  (supposedly) more advanced state, and may happen both in
  and out of physicality

fact – something that supposedly will never change; see opinion

forever – an occurrence of time representing a really, really long
  time; see eternity

form(less) – a consciousness entity spends "time" in form (*Reality*)
  or formless (in *Infinity*)

free thinking – a left-brain / logical approach that fills in missing
  pieces of *Reality*

goal – an end result

God – sometimes equated to the Universe; usually referred to here
  as (invisible) *"Infinity"*

good – acceptable thinking, beliefs, emotions, or outcomes; see bad

gravity – an accepted (agreement) "law" present in our shared *Reality*

happy – an emotional state in which you are satisfied; see miserable

heaven – in Christianity, "good" souls spend an eternity here after
  death; see soul

hell – a concept in Christianity in which "bad" souls spend an
  eternity after death; see soul

human – a consciousness entity holds, and its thinking contains,
  characteristics of the "I think, therefore I am" variety; a
  "branding"

ho'oponopono – an entire system of manifestation based on an ancient Hawaiian tradition (that itself came from elsewhere, and may pre-date "western" religion)

idea – comes from right-brain "thinking" and usually has no precedent; see possibility

imagine (imagination) – totally right-brain emotional "thinking"; see visualize

incarnate – (in-form) when a consciousness entity is incarnate, it is said to be "real" or physical; see form

interpretation (dream) – a meaning assigned via its content

Infinity – a realm where all possibilities reside. It is invisible, includes no words or logic, and is given to be creative. It is similar to "God." It is also the place where all conscious entities reside; see *Reality*

inspiration – "in spirit," often given to come from *Infinity* (right-brain) occurring from your "inside"

intention – a stated belief in a certain outcome; see belief

invisible – something in the *Infinite*, which has not yet appeared as real; referred to in Science of Mind as a spiritual prototype, and by the Law of Attraction as something waiting in escrow to appear; see visible

judgment – as normally applied, a first impression given by something superficial (skin color). Beyond that, we would judge a person as WRONG (making us RIGHT) or just plain stupid (making us smart). Maybe they're simply different; see right, wrong

know(ing) – the most powerful belief; see belief

law – required by existence

base – a law that always applies (gravity)

meta-physics – beyond physics

physics – the physical laws (agreements) that apply to our *Reality*

Law of Attraction (LOA) – a 3-part Law present in all *Realities*, explained best by the channeled source(s) of Abraham

lesson(s) – according to Seth, a consciousness entity will join the physical world for the chance of learning it or them

Life – the process by which things move from the invisible to the visible, the non-physical to the physical, or back

logic – the way the left-brain thinks using words; see reason

lots – used to allude to an infinite # of possibilities

love – both represents: what is usually considered "being in love" with someone ("puppy love"), or the nearest word one can use to express the creative process by *Infinity*

meta-physics – beyond physics; see law, physics

miserable – the opposite of happy; both happiness and misery are caused by yourself

mistake – nothing is given to be a mistake, since we put it all in our script

money $$$ – making a lot is often a goal; but watch out! This goal often comes from outside

movie – our *Life* is often given to be a movie in which we have written the script

multiverse – multiple Universes; see Universe

negative – as used here, "bad"; see positive

New Thought – a religious philosophy in which what is going on, is first experienced as a thought(s) in your mind; it attempts to combine religion and science or right- and left-brain; popular "sects" include Religious Science, Christian Science, and Unity

now – the only place we can actually do anything is now. Some philosophies state it is the only time there is

numerology – a method of developing a reading for your *Life*, based on (the date of) your birth

observe (observation) – used as a synonym for perceive

objective – a term used by Religious Science to refer to the right-brain; see subjective

offense – a negative state one finds himself in because of something presented; remember: no-one else has any power to make you emotional – it is completely under your own power

opinion – an idea (left-brain) about something; it might be the opposite of a fact someone else observes; see fact parent – one who supposedly raises and teaches another human; they are often "blamed" for whatever is wrong in the *Life* of someone they have taught

patent – a legal (left-brain) way to assign a claim over an intangible (right-brain) idea

perception – your view of what is "real" or in *Reality*; see *Reality*

pet – an animal, often kept indoors with you, that is often caused by your consciousness

philosophy – the study of the fundamental nature of knowledge, *Reality*, and existence that is given to "hold together" in total or as a unit; nothing about it is purportedly unexplained

physical – your view of what is "real" or in *Reality*; see *Reality*

physics – a science concerning the "laws" of existence; see law

positive – "good"; see negative

possibility (probability) – in a more coarse "plural" state, it is the invisible collection of all that may become "real" in your experience; it becomes visible in a more refined or personal "singular" state; see idea

promise – a guarantee of completion

program(med) – when your results are determined by teaching or suggestion of someone or something else, usually outside of yourself

prototype – a step in moving something from an idea to a finished product

Quantum Physics – the most current view of Physics explains, through science, how we get what we perceive to be real; see law, perception, physics

Reality – this term is applied to the visible results produced from *Infinity* by *Life*; see *Infinity*, *Life*

reason – the way the left-brain thinks (with words); see logic

refine – a singular or discrete property of related ideas in invisible *Infinity*; this property is often visible in *Reality*

religion – an organized philosophy of *Life* followed by a number of "congregants"

Religious Science – a "New Thought" religion, often known as "Science of Mind" [SOM]

right – when you are on a moral high-road and have judged the other as wrong; see judgment

Roadmap(-of-Life) – a collection of thoughts, events, and emotions representing everything in your *Life*; see Akashic Records

script – when *Life* can be said to be akin to a movie, then we have written the script ourselves; see movie

scripture – tenets of a religion that are written down

Seth (Material) – A channeled body of knowledge

shit – slang that means "bad;" see crap

science – given to left-brain thinking via words, logic, and reason

soul – according to Christianity, you only get one of these and it comes to rest in heaven or hell after the body is in form no longer

spirituality – NOT the same as religion. Everybody has it, like it or not; see religion

spreadsheet – one of several methods by which you may list the positive and negative things (good and bad) in your *Life*, and prioritize what is happening in order you might choose some area(s) to improve

state – implies "static," but here is more of a process, especially where *Life* is concerned. It is derived from the "zero state" (a divine presence only) right before the Big Bang brings everything into existence; see divine

static – unchanging; see state

steal – a judgmental term which means to take without permission

subjective – used by Religious Science to refer to the left-brain mind; see objective

superior – a condition of judgment whereby you feel above another

synchronicity – two (or more) items that occur together or in relation to each other. Nothing is attributed to any cause-and-effect between them

tenet – a belief (religious) expressed in words, and often written

term – the word(s) we use to refer to something

think – we think in our left-brain via words and logic; in the right-brain we think by emotion

time – a relatively recent addition for the left-brain; in our *Reality*, it is forward-going and linear (a version that has one thing occurring after another)

Transcendental Meditation – often referred to as "TM," Transcendental Meditation practitioners demonstrate proof of left- and right-brains via graphs of brain wave scans

tribe – a group to which an individual belongs

UFO – an <u>U</u>nidentified <u>F</u>lying <u>O</u>bject

understand – a process engaged with by the left- (or limited) brain in which understanding is sought via logic or reason. Words are involved

Universe – the collection of everything that is real or visible; at this "time" there is thought to be only one, hence the "Uni"; see Multiverse

victim – you are a victim of something coming from the outside (i.e. someone else suggested it)

view – a particular way of looking at something

visible – an idea appearing "real"; see invisible

visualize – left-brain thinking that requires you or someone else to have done it already; see imagine

wake – the past is steering, as in the wake of a boat is steering it

word(s) – the left-brain uses logic and reason, and thinks using words

worthy – a concept by which you are deserving of something

wrong – when you are in a "bad" state; see judgment

zero state – the state that immediately precedes entry of *Reality* and *Life* (where God, *Infinity*, or the Divine – only – exists)victim – you are a victim of something coming from the outside (i.e. someone else suggested it)

CPSIA information can be obtained
at www.ICGtesting.com
Printed in the USA
LVOW12*1559190318
570339LV00007B/135/P